The Bridal Wave

The Bridal Wave

A SURVIVAL GUIDE TO THE EVERYONE-I-KNOW-IS-GETTING-MARRIED YEARS

· · · · · · · · · · · · · · · · ·

ERIN TORNEO AND
VALERIE CABRERA KRAUSE

Ⓥ VILLARD New York

A Villard Books Trade Paperback Original

Published in the United States by Villard Books,
an imprint of The Random House Publishing Group,
a division of Random House, Inc., New York.

VILLARD and "V" CIRCLED Design are registered
trademarks of Random House, Inc.

ISBN 978-0-8129-7601-4

Printed in the United States of America

www.villard.com

2 4 6 8 9 7 5 3 1

Book design by Jo Anne Metsch

Illustrations by Cheri Messerli

To all of the women who read

the title of this book and

got it instantly

CONTENTS

What Is the Bridal Wave?

Feeling overwhelmed by marriage mania? You aren't alone

One minute, everything is peachy. You are living the independent life you dreamed of in college: you're on your own, nobody tells you what to do or how to do it, and heck, you can blow two weeks' salary on a base-and-highlight if that's what you want. Who needs a husband when you've got a gal pal who'll do power yoga, grocery shopping, and a cheap manicure with you all in one afternoon? Then, *wham!*—you're deluged with engagement parties, shower invites, and save-the-dates. You've got eight weddings to attend, and you can forget that trip to Fiji you've been planning, as weekend after weekend—not to mention paycheck after paycheck—get eaten up. Those friends you counted on for weekend Bloody Mary brunches are busy registering for designer housewares and 1,000-thread-count sheets. Suddenly, you realize you've been stranded on singles' island while they paddle off in rafts made for two with their monogrammed towel sets and the Cuisinart food processor (that you bought them, even though you couldn't afford one for yourself).

The Bridal Wave is the culmination of familial, societal, cultural, and internal pressure to marry that strikes like a tidal wave, sweeping up your friends one by one and showering you with anxieties. The single, carefree life that you once celebrated is suddenly called into question at every turn. Conversations start to relentlessly revolve around who's getting married next or who might be on the verge of engagement. If you're not next in line, it's easy to feel like the odd woman out. You may be in grad school kicking ass, you may be flying up the corporate ladder in your dream job, or you may be having the time of your life just trying to find your way. But if you don't have a ring around a certain finger or (gasp!) aren't even in the running by a certain age, people are going to start asking: "Why aren't you seeing anyone?" or "Have you tried online dating?" followed by the gentle suggestion that you lower your standards: "What about Dan in Payroll? He's been looking a lot better since that rash cleared up." Or you attend your younger sister's wedding without a date and *someone else's* relatives try to set you up with "nice boys." The not-so-subtle subtext is screaming, "You aren't getting any younger!" And how about those looks of forced enthusiasm when your married friends decide that you "need to get out there" and plan the dreaded Girls' Night Out, where they sit nursing a Cosmo and encouraging you to chat up the dweeb at the bar, all the while silently thanking their lucky solitaires that they don't have to?

Being single can suck when you're made to feel like some kind of social leper for not having a serious boyfriend, but the fact is, even if you've got a guy you aren't free from the wrath of the Bridal Wave. Those of us in relationships also face the firing squad, sometimes in a more overt way—like when your family corners you at Thanksgiving dinner and asks flat out, "When are you two going to make it official?" or your friends attack you after you return from vacation to see if he popped the question. Others will sneak a peak at your hand after a weekend in Vermont, Valentine's Day, or any other engagement-appropriate occasion, then look up from your suddenly naked-feeling finger with eyes that say, "Not this time either, huh?"

But far and away, the most tormenting voice is the one in our own heads. When this first Bridal Wave strikes, usually in your mid-twenties, panic can set in. Formerly happy, sane, accomplished women turn insecure and desperate. Some among us decide to find a mate with as much tenacity as we pursue our MBAs. We buy bridal magazines and plan the ceremony down to the napkin rings even though there's no groom in the picture; or we hint continuously to our boyfriends (many of whom aren't even worthy of us, truth be told). You may not even be sure you want to get married, but the point is, *why the hell isn't he asking?!* Racing thoughts at night fill our mind with unanswerable questions (though our parents, friends, and oftentimes complete strangers seem perfectly clear on what we need to do).

Or maybe you wake up one day and realize that thirty is bearing down on you like a Mack truck and according to the life plan you concocted when you were twenty, you should already be married. Your up-till-now-happy relationship is subject to severe scrutiny: *Is he the one? Is there even time to meet a new one? We've been together for three years already, so I can't just scrap the whole thing now.*

We've been there. We get it. And we're here to say that enough is enough! It's time for a backlash. Not a backlash against marriage. Marriage is wonderful if that is what you want and if you have found the right person. After all, the pharmaceutical companies make it look so nice in their TV ads—two silver-haired people pushing seventy, holding hands and walking along the beach, sharing a lifetime of memories and, apparently, the benefits of the latest arthritis drug. We mean a backlash against the insanity. Against women feeling pressure to wed because they are sucked into the Bridal Wave—they don't want to be last, they don't want to be alone, they want to start a family, they want to "beat" a friend who seems to do everything first and better, they don't want to be the scary cat lady, or they're conforming to a timeline they created when they were fifteen years old.

Most of us could sing the chorus to "You Can't Hurry Love" and "Que Será Será," but for many of us take-charge, control-your-own-destiny types, this sit-back-and-let-life-happen philosophy is a hard pill to swallow. To get into a good college, we took SAT prep. To get those shoes that we can't live without, we whip out our plastic and charge them. We're used to going for what we want. "It's really frustrating not knowing if it's ever going to happen to you," says Karen, thirty-two, one of the many brave, gracious, gorgeous gals who shared their stories with us. "The lack of control is horrifying. It makes you feel really girly and disempowered."

We're going to help you stay sane when you're neck deep in other people's nuptials and your own inner turmoil. Why? Because we know a little something about it—and even though you feel like you're the *only* one you know who isn't getting hitched any time soon, you aren't alone. We sit on different sides of the great nuptial divide, but we're both survivors of the Bridal Wave. This book is going to give you strategies and tips to ride the wave on your own terms.

From Erin

I was always the girl who knew when to cut and run. If a relationship was obviously not working out, I ended it and never looked back. But something changed in my mid-twenties. Engagement announcements, shower invites, and save-the-dates were all starting to flood my mailbox. They seemed to signal "Entering Adulthood," and apparently I had some catching up to do. The guys I dated started bringing up the M-word as the inevitable next step, so I figured these were serious relationships that I had to invest time and effort in. Instead of throwing in the towel, I thought it was my job to fix what, looking back, were totally unfixable relationships. Like the trustafarian who claimed he was covering our expensive entrées at a group birthday dinner, only to shortchange all of my friends who ordered the pasta. Or the poet who developed a fake online identity and tried to seduce underage girls with verse he penned for me. Or how about that lying letch who wound up in some stewardess's hotel room, taking seminude photos of her, which I was supposed to understand because it was all for his "art"?

What I missed while I was so busy trying to salvage these relationships was the fact that they weren't even marriageworthy to begin with. If I had headed down the aisle when I thought I was supposed to because everyone I knew was making the trip—and hell, when I was younger, twenty-six sounded like the "right" age to be married—I would absolutely be divorced by now.

Thankfully, I came to my senses and reclaimed my singledom. Sure, it was rough in more than a few places for a while, but eventually I was okay with being on my own. I had great friends and family, a job I loved that let me travel the world, and then, sure enough, I met my current boyfriend. Finally, I have a fully functional relationship with a great guy, whom my friends actually like and invite to group functions. (And here I had always thought that they preferred to keep things girls-only. Now I know that they had actually just hated my exes.)

You'd think being in a loving relationship would stop the insanity, right? Wrong. At weddings we get questions like "So would you two have a big wedding or would you elope?" It's tough to stay confident when you are constantly explaining your relationship to other people: "No, we are not married or engaged, but yes, we are happy and plan on staying together." When enough people have asked you why you and your boyfriend aren't married yet, it's hard not to start asking yourself the same question and skewering your own relationship.

My boyfriend and I have gone to twelve—twelve!— weddings together so far and have five more this year, two of which are my brothers'. While one would think having two family weddings (three if you count my cousin) would ease the pressure, it only seems to have made things worse. That my younger brother is taking the plunge—and I'm cohabitating—fuels the fire. Mom "happens" to find her wedding dress one weekend while I'm home to visit; at a large family dinner, Dad says things like "I have a feeling there's going to be another wedding next year." He winks, I cringe.

Don't get me wrong, it's not that I don't want to marry my boyfriend. It's just that these winks and comments pile up in my head and reawaken the Cinderella fantasy I buried long ago. And then the freak-out begins. For example, what if he doesn't propose this year? Does that mean he's never going to? Have I ruined it because we moved in together? Why do these things matter when I'm not even sure I want a wedding? And if I don't care about weddings, why did I get weepy watching the InStyle Weddings special in a Montreal hotel room (dubbed in French, no less, which I don't speak a word of)?

I'm having a hard time figuring out exactly what I want when so many people have a vested interest in seeing me married off. It's like I'm the solitary holdout among legions of the wedded who won't rest until I've come over to their side. More and more, I find myself playing defense at weddings, gearing up for the inevitable questions and inaudible murmurings. While most of my peers have ceased with the bouquet toss (it's more like "Pass me the baton and let's call it a day already"), now I'm facing round two of weddings, the next generation. Nothing like getting dragged out for the bouquet toss and sharing the floor with giggling teenage girls and someone's thrice-divorced, heavily

Botoxed aunt, right? Sometimes my reasons for wanting to tie the knot are crazy: so I can give the finger (my ring finger, of course!) to all the inappropriate questions forever, plus we can get some Wüsthof knives out of the deal.

This is the book I wish had been available to me when I ended the relationship with the man I thought was "the one" in a back room of the banquet facility where my best friend had just gotten married. This is the book I wish I could have found when another friend got married and her Old World Italian uncle said to me, "Whatta you gonna do now Emily married? Whya you no married, eh?" This is the book I hope will help you every time you pick up a voice mail message that says, "I've got big news."

From Valerie

I was not the girl who woke up for the Charles-and-Di wedding. My Barbies got it on with Ken, but they never married him. I played army, not princess. But the years of not caring about walking down the aisle ended for me in one fell swoop. At the age of twenty-four my friend Tracey got married. Hers was the first wedding in our friendship circle. And while Tracey was prepping and trying to gather her nerves before the ceremony, we, her single girlfriends, who had no idea how to help her, spied her veil. One by one, we tried it on like little girls playing dress-up. We each took a turn admiring ourselves in the mirror and even took photos of each other playing Bride.* You hear about women holding a baby and realizing that they just have to be a mom—well, when I donned that veil I knew that what I really wanted was to get married, and not just because I looked so fantastic in it. The wedding was moving, and seeing Tracey and Brian as happy as they were together made me feel something that I hadn't expected: jealousy. I felt like Veruca Salt: I want a dress! I want a wedding! I want to call someone my husband!

I was twenty-four, not dating anyone, and in fact I had never had a real boyfriend, so really, what business did I have trying on veils and going all Veruca? Not only was I not next in line, I wasn't in the lineup at all! You know the girl that other girls hang out with when they want a "fun night out" or they are in between boyfriends? That was me. I was the girl who had a ton of boy friends, but not a lot of boyfriends. (Hookups don't count.) Being the perma-single girl of all my friends had never been my favorite role. Before Tracey's wedding I didn't sweat it much. I was young, having fun, and "dating around," even if most of my dates were one-hit wonders. I wasn't really sure of what I wanted in life, but that wedding changed things for me.

As more of my friends began coupling up, my single status became a sore topic for me. I didn't want to be the fifth wheel anymore. Every new bit of engagement

*No joke. View the photos on our website, www.thebridalwave.com.

news became a reminder that not only would my credit card be taking a $100 hit (minimum, not including tax or shipping), but that I was alone and falling behind.

Then I met Tommy and we moved in together after dating for a year. At the time, I was working at an advertising agency, which was staffed mostly by women under thirty. Weddings, you can probably guess, were the hot topic. One by one girls were getting engaged. I learned what the "4 Cs" were (cut! clarity! carat! and color!), I learned that it is best to register at Crate and Barrel, because they let you return gifts under $100 for cash (not that I returned any of my gifts, of course!), and I was hell-bent on not being the last one there to get a ring. Thus began Ring Watch 2001: The watch I got for my birthday? Not a ring. The necklace I got for our dating anniversary? Not a ring. The surprise trip to Hawaii? Nope, not a ring.

What had happened to me? The same thing I see happening to women all the time. I have friends who are single and happy—happy until their mom asks them if they are a lesbian; happy until they hear that for every IQ point above average they are, the less likely they are to get married; happy until they get sucked into the pink section of the bookstore, filled with books promising to help them plan the perfect wedding or else find Mr. Right and then plan the perfect wedding. Then I have a friend who was happy with her boyfriend and not thinking about marriage until he handed her a blue box for Christmas (which contained *a platinum band with diamonds on it) and said, "This isn't an engagement ring." Merry Christmas!*

I am writing this book for all of them. Not just for the girl who has a stack of bridal magazines in her closet, or the girl who has a wedding binder with torn-out magazine pages of flowers, colors, and gift ideas "just in case," or the girl who TiVos A Wedding Story. Even the most independent young women can find themselves caught up in the Bridal Wave. This book is not about getting a man, keeping a man, or marrying a man. This is about keeping the crazies in check.

ARE YOU AT RISK?

Here are the most common criteria of
Bridal Wavus Overwhelmus.

☑ When you get together with friends, you find your eyes glazing over as they discuss fittings, floral arrangements, and the advantages of buffet style.

☑ You could, if forced to do so, describe two bridal shower games.

☑ You have been pulled out to the dance floor against your will to play "catch the bouquet."

☑ You can name three celebrity engagements from the past two years (it's okay if they're already divorced).

☑ Your grandparents' favorite conversation topics are Social Security, hip replacement surgery, and your flatlining love life.

☑ You keep asking yourself why your money is so tight even though you haven't splurged on a trip or a bag you loved in a long time.

☑ You have heard "You'll be able to wear this dress again" more times than you care to count.

☑ You have looked at an engaged friend and thought to yourself, *How is she getting married while I'm still single?*

☑ You have felt at least once as if your engaged/married friends feel sorry for you because you are still single.

☑ You worry that you will be the last of your friends to get married.

If you have experienced more than half of these symptoms, it is our duty to inform you that you are caught in the Bridal Wave. But hang on, sister. Help is on the way!

The Bridal Wave

"I've Got Big News!"

Even my college roommate with Tourette's has a ring!
What to do when someone's "big news"
means a meltdown for you

You're in your mid-twenties. Your oldest friend gets engaged.
Then your sorority sister. Then the girl who was gay (apparently only until graduation). Life as you know it is over. Every
time you check your messages and you hear, "I've got big news"
you know what it means: another friend has signed off the single life—the itch-to-hitch epidemic has struck again.

The first few times you hear this news, you're probably unfazed. Going to a wedding of your peers is still a novelty, and it
seems decidedly grown-up. But as more and more of your
posse get proposals, what had been a sign of adulthood for all
of you may begin to feel more like being picked last for the
kickball team all over again. You look at the girl who made the
cut just ahead of you and wonder, "Am I really the worst player
here?"

Yes, it's unavoidable that at some point in your first or second
wave of weddings (there are usually two, the group of people
who go for the gold—or platinum—in their early to mid-
twenties, and another group that comes down with matrimania

in their late twenties to thirties), you will start to question your own life. It could be at any point in the engagement process: the actual IGBN call, the bridal shower when all of the married women talk about how great it is to be married, the bachelorette party where you are reminded of how horrible it is to go to cheesy clubs and do shots all night, or maybe even the actual wedding itself. As you watch your friends walk down the aisle, you feel happy for them and glad that they have found each other, but at the same time you're reminded that it hasn't happened for you yet. You wonder if it's ever going to. Are you going to meet "the one" (we *hate* that phrase)—that elusive somebody who will want the same things you want and think it's cute when you wake up with pillow tracks on one side of your face? You look at the date you've brought and think, "*He's* not it, either." And then the self-spin cycle clicks on: you obsess over the decisions you've made, the ones who got away, or the ones that you missed by getting back together (again) with that one guy who worms his way back into your life, each time just long enough for you to remember why you ended it with him last time.

When Andrea, twenty-seven, used to go to weddings in her early twenties, she was quite the scene-stealer: "I'd realize that my boyfriend and I weren't even close to the couple up on the altar getting married. Then I'd drink a lot and get belligerent—I was always fighting back tears." Maybe all those who claim "I cry at weddings" aren't exactly weeping tears of joy but rather conveniently covering up feelings of envy, competition, and brutal self-examination.

It's only natural to think of your own life when you hear someone else's good news. Especially because up until now,

From Erin

I remember getting stuck in an airport due to snow-storms one January during a cross-country flight. I checked my voice mail. One new message: an IGBN from my best friend since the first grade. As I dialed her number in the parka-stuffed crowd of stranded travelers, I steadied myself against my carry-on. "Well, Bob and I . . ." she began. Did I even actually hear the rest? I gave her my best wishes, listened to the story of how he proposed (it was a good story—the writer in me knew that), and felt genuinely happy for her. But I hung up with a big lump in my throat. I felt hot, claustrophobic, and achingly lonely at the same time: my best friend was getting married. Meanwhile, I was only three months into the worst breakup of my life. I was convinced that I had missed much more than my plane connection. I had missed the boat.

we've shared our life stages with most of our friends and had some modicum of control over what happened next in our lives. Everyone takes driver's ed and gets a license at sixteen; everyone studies and graduates high school and heads off to college at the same time. There you battle the freshman fifteen with your dorm mates, get an internship, impress some people, and land a job. But love and marriage? Well, even us little Type As can't force someone to marry us (at least not legally). Not only can't you hurry love, but honey, you can't even *plan* for it.

Add to that the domino effect of your friends heading down

the aisle in droves, outfitting their homes with Tiffany salt and pepper shakers and Calphalon pots and pans while you're still using your hand-me-downs from your old roomie (who moved out when she got engaged), and you can start to feel a bit like the Lone Ranger who got left behind when Tonto found his true love and ran off. Your mismatched, chipped plates and dishes are a glaring reminder that everyone else is now adults, with matching place settings and luggage. But nothing truly triggers the four-alarm fire like running into your secret rival and having her flash the ice on her left hand with a ~~victorious~~ lovestruck gleam in her eye. Ain't competition a bitch?

"Damn It, How Did She Beat Me at This, Too?"

Amy, twenty-four, is recovering from a full-on Frenemy attack: she and her long-distance boyfriend, Joel, were doing great—she expected he might propose "anytime now." They had discussed their future and knew that "I do"s were in it. All good, right? Well, it would have been perfect except for the fact that her friend Jessica once again upstaged her. Meet the Frenemy: the one girl who you've felt inferior to your whole life. The Frenemy plays a crucial role in an IGBN wig-out. In Amy's case, her longtime Frenemy, Jessica, started dating her boyfriend a few months *after* Amy and Joel got together, yet Jessica and her beau got engaged after dating for only six months. "We have known each other since we were five, and our parents are great friends. But no matter what I did growing up, Jess did it better. In high school we both played violin, but she had to go and *major* in music. Then she dated my ex and all I heard was

'They're the perfect couple.' *Great,* I thought, *even my ex likes her better than me.* I thought that I finally had her beat when it came to saying 'I do' and just once, I could be the center of attention. But she won again." Of course, getting engaged to outdo someone is not a smart idea. For all she knows, Jessica's going to be first at other things too, like say, getting divorced. Amy told us repeatedly how "ridiculous" she knew she was for feeling this way, yet she couldn't help herself.

Sweet and Polite on the Outside; Envious, Resentful, and Threatened Deep Down

We know how we are *supposed* to feel when we hear someone else's good news: we are supposed to smile, congratulate them, and wish them all the best. In our survey,* 77 percent of the women who responded said that getting the call from a friend had made them feel stressed about their own love life, jealous that they weren't the one headed to the altar, or worried that they would be the last to get hitched. And having this self-awareness only makes us feel even worse about our real feelings of envy, anxiety, and self-pity. Most of the women we talked to described these not-so-attractive reactions as "ridiculous," "ugly," or just plain "yucky." Despite the ick factor, these reactions are totally normal, especially when you think about the scare tactics we've grown up with. Just one of the more notable gems from the infamous 1986 *Newsweek* article "If You're a Single Woman, Here Are Your Chances of Getting Married" was the oft-quoted statistic

*The Bridal Wave online survey, hosted by Survey Monkey.

that a forty-year-old woman has a better chance of being killed by a terrorist than tying the knot.

Sound familiar? For a generation that grew up with headlines about "man shortages," every woman is a potential rival. Plus, as if being last didn't suck enough already, it followed that any stragglers would have even slimmer pickings of potential mates. And let's not get started on the guys of a certain age who reset their dating radar to *younger* women.

Here's what we say about the inner Tonya Harding who surfaces when you feel like you're losing your competitive edge: marriage is not a race. Getting to the altar is not crossing a finish line but merely the beginning of another leg. Try to channel that competitive energy into making yourself a happier person. Yes, it's hokey to say it, but indulging jealousy is a waste of time. To calm the beast:

- **Mad-lib it.** Think of three things that you have/do/are that you'd never trade for her life. Need a jump start? We've made it easy. Just fill in the blanks: "She may be engaged, but I have way better [insert noun] than she and she can't [insert verb] as well as I can, and let's face it, she wishes that she were as [insert adjective] as I am."

- **Play to win.** Still feeling the rage? Focus your competitive instincts on an actual competition, like a 10K race, a walkathon, or a good game of poker.

- **Picture this.** How about going through your iPhoto and actually getting some of your pictures off your computer and into some frames? Not only is it productive, but also it'll be a nice little trip down memory lane so you can remind yourself that your life has actually been pretty sweet.

- **Celebrate yourself.** Make your own IGBN calls. Got a big promotion? Invite people out to toast your success. Moving into a new pad? Throw yourself a housewarming. Just because you don't get to register doesn't mean you can't get gifts.

From Val

My IGBN meltdown happened when I was twenty-six. My boyfriend and I were in what my father called our "year of playing house," and I was forced to deal with my equally engagement-obsessed co-worker Bonnie on a daily basis. Bonnie and I were neck and neck: we were both in serious relationships, we both moved in with our boyfriends, and we had both had "The Talk," as planned. So now we were both ladies in waiting: waiting for our boyfriends to pick their moment.

Some women propose to their men. Good for them and for their superevolved selves. Tommy does the laundry and the dishes and is a better cook than me, but when I teased him about how I was going to propose, he let me know that he would not be okay with that. And truthfully I wouldn't have been, either. Why not? Call me a traditionalist, but when I thought of getting engaged, the scene had a man on bended knee, not me. So when Bonnie came back from her vacation sporting a rock, I was thrilled for her, of course. But there was that other side of me that was furious that her guy had asked her first. What was Tommy's problem? Why was he taking so long? If it hadn't been for Bonnie's matrimania, in which I was completely complicit, I'm not sure my panic would have been so intense. Instead of keeping each other above the hitching hysteria, we were dragging each other under.

Unfortunately, there's no fancy cream or spa treatment to make these feeling of anxiety go away. How you choose to deal with them is up to you. You can:

1. Feel sorry for yourself and spend a weekend in your PJs with your remote control and snack of choice, leaving your house only to get frozen yogurt.
2. Bitch to your friends about how you are never going to find anyone, then refuse to take any of their advice about meeting new people.
3. Go out to dinner with a fellow ringless friend and go back and forth discussing how it is unbelievable that no one has scooped the other up considering how hot, smart, and funny you both are.
4. Focus on renewing your single-friend friendships. Go out, get rip-roaring drunk, and flirt with a younger guy, just to know that you still got it. (Safe hookups and no drunk driving, please.)

5. Think of something you enjoy doing but don't do enough of. Loved kayaking on that family vacation you took ten years ago? Become the Queen of Kayaking.

6. Pick something that you are unhappy with that is within your control, and change it. Hate your job? Get your résumé in order, call a headhunter, and get the heck out of there.

7. Relearn something that you have forgotten. Honestly, how much of your French do you remember? Sign up for a refresher course, or, better yet, go online and find someone who is willing to trade lessons with you.

We recommend doing a bit of all of the above. There's *nothing* wrong with a night in and your favorite must-see TV. Likewise, if all of your friends are headed for the Fondue Club thanks to their registries, make new friends with some like-minded single women.

• Having single gal pals is the first step in protecting yourself against the hell of the Bridal Wave. You need to be able to call in backup and spill your guts about how you really feel.

• If you have a small circle of close friends, make a new friend who is as far from the circle as possible. She'll be completely on your side (because she won't have any loyalty to your other friends). Another bonus: you can talk as much trash about your Club Wedd friends as you like and they'll never hear a word of it. It's a handy way to stay off the gossip trail while still finding an outlet for your feelings.

Listen Up, Ladies!

Swallowing your anger will only lead to a Pompeii-esque eruption. And since you never know when you'll blow, best to let off some steam every now and then. After all, freaking out in the middle of a wedding reception? Not so great when someone digs out that always-entertaining wedding video.

Charlize Has Nothing on You

Relying on friends is a great way to manage anxiety overall, but what about when you are in the heat of the moment? Even if you're excited for your friend, an IGBN call can feel like a sucker punch, especially when it's coming from your best bud (you thought she'd be with you until the end!). Honesty is the best policy for most things in life, but when it comes to taking The Call, take our word for it: fake it! The minute you feel your heart sink and your blood pressure rise, go on autopilot and act like you're over the moon. Give an award-worthy performance (it doesn't have to be Oscar material; Golden Globe will do).

It could be your eighth IGBN call of the year, or your boyfriend may have just told you that he is interested in an "open relationship," or you may have just realized that your first-year anniversary of being dateless is coming up, but for your friend or sister, or even the annoyingly ambitious girl you've sorta hated since high school, just fake it. Remember, this is a once in a lifetime moment for her, so put a sock in your selfish self. Don't be Bitter Girl. Believe it or not, women remember how their friends reacted to their good news.

Why Faking It Can Be the Best Approach to the IGBN Call: Bitter Soup

Liz had been dating her live-in boyfriend, Mike, for nearly eight years. Just about everyone, including their mailman, knew she wanted him to pop the question. She would check out the De Beers website "just for fun" on Mike's computer *and bookmarked* the site for his edification. She would tease Mike about how all of her friends, who had been their single friends at the beginning of their relationship, were now all getting hitched. Of course there was nothing fun about this teasing, and all of her friends wished that he would just propose already.

Liz was hosting Thanksgiving for her friends, an annual tradition. Every year Mike would carve the turkey while Liz looked on blissfully, imagining herself in a suburban home with a white picket fence, rather than the one-bedroom she and Mike shared in Queens. Just before they sat down to dinner, the phone rang. Liz answered, listened for a moment, and turned to the room and announced with all the emotion of a subway conductor, "Susannah and Andy are engaged." Susannah's other friends were superexcited and eager to hear the details from Susannah herself. But instead of passing the phone, Liz said to Susannah abruptly, "That's great, but dinner's ready and the soup is getting cold," and then hung up; that's right, she hung up. There was an uncomfortable silence as Liz went about ladling the soup as if nothing had happened. She was obviously internally combusting over the fact that yet another couple had sealed the deal while she sat back and waited. Among Susannah's friends, that day is still referred to as "the great soup incident of 2003."

When you are caught off guard by an engagement announcement, remember the stock phrase "I'm so happy for you" and use it so you won't go down in history as a horrible bitch or say something that could hurt your friendship.

Another Tactic: Keep 'Em Talking

If you find yourself tongue-tied or tempted to rattle off the latest divorce stats, keep her talking so you don't have to. People love to talk about themselves. This rule is good to remember for your next job interview or dinner party, but especially true of a woman planning a wedding. Once you've got a newly engaged woman started, all you have to do is say a word or two that gives her the green light to keep going ("Oh?!" and "Really?!" both work). She'll remember you as a caring, interested friend while you catch up on your tweezing.* Here are some conversation starters:

---

*It goes without saying that you are a sensitive, smart woman who loves her friends. We're just trying to keep you from going nuts.

☎ *"Tell me all about the proposal. Was it everything you thought it would be?"*

☎ *"Have you thought of where you will have the ceremony? How about the reception? Places book up so fast these days, you know."*

☎ *Have you given any thought to your wedding palette? What colors are hot this year?*

☎ *Where will you be honeymooning? You know, where you go is so important!*

☎ *Have you set up any bridal boutique appointments yet? You don't want to get a rush charge.*

☎ *Have you thought about what kind of favor you will give your guests?*

Not only will these conversation starters allow you time to concentrate on your hangnails, they will really get her mind racing. She will realize how much there is to learn—how many decisions to make and how much time and energy she is about to devote to one day of her life. Of course, we would never advocate trying to stress out your friend on purpose—not us! But after all, isn't it your duty as a caring friend to see to it that nothing falls through the cracks? You are really just "being there" for her, right?

Postcall Panic Do's and Don'ts

After you hang up the phone and begin to wonder how even *she* is getting hitched and before your mind begins to spin out of control:

✓ Do call a like-minded singleton (preferably one who can boost your spirits).

✗ Don't kill a bottle of Chardonnay and drunk-dial your exes.

✓ Do make plans to go out and celebrate your ability to be totally spontaneous. Your friends who are hurrying to get hitched won't be doing much of that.

✗ Don't sit on your couch watching basic cable.

Believe It or Knot

Before all this talk of happily ever after, there was an ancient tradition called "marriage by capture." Basically, the groom-to-be needed close friends and family to function like a small army when he fought off angry family members and kidnapped his intended, hence his "best men." Bridesmaids became more common later, and one of their duties was to dress like the bride, while the groomsmen were outfitted (not much changed here!) just like the groom at the ceremony. The reason? The bridal party would be like decoys, just in case evil spirits or jealous suitors attempted to harm the newlyweds. So think about that the next time someone asks you to do the honors.[1]

The Friendship Dump

She's your best friend, but now she has a new best friend, and she's marrying him. It feels like getting dumped. As if you weren't feeling lonely enough, now you don't have the best friend you used to always count on. When your best bud gets engaged, it's a neon sign flashing: You are no longer her top priority! You can no longer assume she's in when you snag two fare-saver tickets to Brazil on a whim! Not only will she be busy planning a wedding, but she's also making her guy her family. He's going to come before you, despite the fact that you've known her since you were six.

Yup, you're going to have to make adjustments in your friendship because of some bozo. The reality of wedding planning means that even the coolest, least princessy chick is going to be up to her ears in floral arrangements, cake tastings, and DJ "do *not* play" lists, which means that she's going to be less available to you. But if it's a longtime pal, your friendship has likely endured some changes before (like say, her unfortunate post-college Goth stage), and it will weather this too. Four friendship-saving tips:

- **Grant her a reprieve.** While she is in the midst of planning hell, give her six months to play B2B but don't cut her out of your life. Make it easy to see her by volunteering to help with some of the planning. Together you can make even the dreariest of errands fun, right?

- **Be honest.** Tell her you miss hanging out with her; chances are she's going to miss her single days from time to time and will relish some girl time, sans her man.

- **Try a threesome.** Not *that* kind of threesome! Try to find a way to hang with both of them. This guy is going to be around for a while, and if you can find a way to have a relationship with him, you'll probably get to see your girl more often.

- **Adjust.** You can't expect her to be the same girl who stumbled home at 8 A.M. with you after clubbing in Madrid. Actually, she still *is* that girl, but her new hubby probably won't take too kindly to a reprise of your backpacking through Europe days. Meet somewhere in the middle—we don't mean you should be stuck playing Pictionary with a bunch of boring couples forever—but maybe meet at a bar for happy hour every few weeks to catch up.

Of course, it's one thing to get an IGBN, but the call takes on a whole new dimension when a person you care about announces her engagement to someone you've always been less than thrilled about.

What to Do When You Feel Like Your Friend Is Making a Mistake

We've all had some dating doozies that we can chalk up conveniently to the whole "love is blind" thing. Our friends are there to back us up, so if we're messing around with some guy who's subpar, they may bite their tongues and hope we come to our senses before we find ourselves anywhere near a church. But what do we do when a friend is altar-bound with some guy who we think is all wrong?

WHY DON'T YOU LIKE HIM?

1. His personality is about as sparkling as twenty-year-old linoleum.
2. You find his habit of shouting out sports trivia annoying.
3. He is a major deadbeat who has been sponging off her for years.
4. You fear she's rushing, trying to beat an arbitrary deadline she set for herself.
5. You've seen him hit on other women.

If you answered 1 or 2: You're going to have to deal. He may not warm the cockles of your heart—especially since he has co-opted the time she used to spend with you—but if he's a decent guy who makes your friend happy and treats her well, zip it. Otherwise, you may end up putting her into a situation where she has to choose. Your BFF pledge notwithstanding, she will, after all, legally vow to spend the rest of her life with him.

If you answered 3–5: You are about to enter shaky ground.

- **Confer.** Talk to your mutual friends and see if they have the same concerns about the guy. This way, you'll know if you are alone in thinking that the guy is a dud. If they strongly agree, it might be best to talk to her as a group, intervention-style.
- **Nominate a spokesperson.** If you know that she's going to feel ganged up on, decide who has the best chance of having a heart-to-heart in the caring way it's intended. Some people are better at broaching sensitive topics than others, and everyone's relationship is different. If you are close enough to her to be this worried, then you probably know the best way to approach her.

- **Avoid an adversarial tone.** Just let her know that you all really care about her and are worried that she isn't seeing some of the issues in her relationship that could blow up down the line.
- **Don't alienate her.** Even if your friend makes what you think is a terrible decision, there isn't a whole lot of satisfaction in saying "I told you so" if her marriage tanks. Mistakes may be made, but in the end, she's going to need her friends.

Listen Up, Ladies!

If the guy is in any way emotionally or physically abusive, or if he has a substance abuse problem, you should not beat around the bush. The stress of a new engagement or impending marriage is a pressure cooker for already simmering problems. Talk to your friend and let her know why you're worried. If she's deep in denial, you may want to call a professional for advice. Look online for resources and call a hotline. (Two places to start: the National Domestic Violence Hotline at www.ndvh.org/800-799-SAFE, and Al-Anon at www.al-anon.org/888-4Al-Anon.) Or, if you feel comfortable doing so, call her family and speak with them. Be forewarned that this act could be the end of your friendship. She may resent you going behind her back to her family or accuse you of being jealous, but speaking your mind now is more important for her well-being in the long run.

The IGBN call is just the tip of the iceberg, which is probably why we come to dread it so much. It is the start of our questioning if we're really where we wanted to be and if we are ever going to be, and it's the beginning of a major shift in our lives toward true-blue adulthood. In our twenties and thirties, we're like each other's boyfriends. We're never alone because we have each other to call, go to the movies with, commiserate about our crap jobs, or toast each other's successes. That is, until certain traitors start replacing us with hairier, stinkier specimens with zero respect for the cleanse, exfoliate, moisturize regimen. Nothing is stranger than watching a woman get engaged. "It's like they transform into wives as soon as they get a ring. They just play the role," says Angelina.

Repeat After Us

I promise to be fake in the face of yet another IGBN call. I will ooh and ahh over a friend's engagement ring, even if I am 100 percent certain that it is cubic zirconia. I will hold my tongue when my Frenemy buys the wedding dress that I had pointed out to her as "my dream dress"—although I will later bitch to my other friends about it and revel in their empathy. I will remember what's good in my life instead of what's good in hers for as long as we both shall live. I will keep my conversation starters handy, so I can carry on the bridal convo while giving myself a pedicure and watching whatever crappy show I want to watch, because I am single and nobody tells me not to do my toes on the couch. I will resist the urge to demand that my friend return her half of the gold heart best-friend charm I gave her in junior high while screaming, "Was I just a placeholder in your life until you found a partner?" I will smile politely when she starts acting all wifey and not remind her that she used to say marriage was an outdated concept for less evolved people. I will do this because she is my friend and I love her, but I will not stand back if I have proof that the slime she wants to marry is getting some on the side.

CHAPTER 2

Lobridemized!

When your friend becomes a bridal drone:
why it happens and how your friendship
can survive her engagement

Losing a bud to the other side sucks for most singletons, but when she suddenly seems like a complete stranger, it's downright freaky. And no, we are not talking about Bridezilla, that she-monster of matrimonial anticipation who barks orders at everyone from the day her engagement is announced to the end of her reception in her quest to be the perfect princess bride. While your friend isn't throwing temper tantrums about peonies that *must* be flown in from Paris, she may exhibit another upsetting malady: the lobridemy. This temporary condition strikes suddenly, short-circuiting the betrothed's brain waves. Her connection to reality is replaced by a connection to all things connubial. A lobridemy can occur at any point along the road to "I do," though victims are usually expected to make a full recovery after the last thank-you note has been sent out. The lobridemized rarely do physical damage to themselves or others, but their unrelenting bridal blather can certainly put a strain on even the best of friendships.

When her close college friend got married, Angela was more

than a little bummed. "Lauren was my party girl. All through college, she refused to get a boyfriend. 'Why get tied down?' was her main refrain. She was a total blast to be with. After college, she moved back home to Florida. Within three months, she was dating someone. Great, I thought. In nine months, they moved in together. I was totally happy for her. At a year, he gave her a ring. She begged me to come visit, but when I got there, all she wanted to do was run wedding-related errands, read wedding-related magazines, and discuss wedding-related topics. She wasn't going Bridezilla on anyone, but I was like, *Who are you and what have you done with my friend?*"

It's Not Her Fault! Understanding Why Even the Smartest Women Can Become Lobridemized

No, you're not being oversensitive; she *has* become a dull, self-centered drone. But is she to blame for her condition? Most of her craziness is the direct result of the wedding industry. Larger than the GNP of some small nations, the *$125 billion* the wedding industry rakes in annually is a profit margin that can steamroll even the strongest of women. The equation is simple really:

Lots of cash + pressure to be unique + once in a lifetime event + a judge and jury of your family and friends = lobridemy in the making

Just how does the wicked WIC (wedding-industrial complex) trap its prey? Let's take a look into the madness—not only will it possibly save your friendship, but there's takeaway value for you, the Bridal Wave victim. When people are asking *you* your thoughts on formal versus casual china someday, you'll hear the "ka-ching!" right away. For now, try to get yourself into the head of the B2B. This should make you psyched to be single!

How would you deal with it . . .

- **if you were constantly being ripped off?** Forty-three percent of couples confess that they dropped more dough than they had planned, which is no surprise considering experiences like Danielle's updo don't: "I called a fancy salon to get a quote on an updo for my wedding day. I almost choked when they said five hundred dollars. The next day I was telling my friend, who thought it was total BS. She called them back and asked how much it would be for an updo for an event she had coming up. They told her $250!"

- **if you were pouring money into stuff you just learned how to pronounce?** With the average cost of a wedding in the United States estimated at just under $27,000 for 2006[1] (though that figure is easily tripled in urban areas), your friend is spending more money on one day than she may make annually. On the next page is a categorical breakdown along with a few ideas of what else could be done with the same funds.

- **if you were trying to figure out how to break even on your investment, or better yet, come out ahead?** Target's

Amount Spent[2]	Wedding Purchase	Parent-Sanctioned Purchase	You-Only-Live-Once Purchase
$1,841	Attire (bride and groom)	Mac 15" laptop	Flat-screen HDTV
$2,337	Ceremony	Drop $2000 into your IRA (blow the remaining $337 on whatever you want)	European vacation (this time without the backpacks)
$1,104	Wedding favors and gifts	A suit "for the position you want, not the position you have"	A trip to Vegas; bet on black
$2,659	Photography and video	A new couch (you aren't fooling anyone with your "ethnic" Urban Outfitters throw—we still smell the cat pee)	A four-nights Spa Sampler package at Canyon Ranch
$13,692	Reception	Take a chunk out of your grad school loans	Spring cleaning in style: throw out all your clothes, hire a personal shopper, and get a brand new wardrobe
$809	Wedding stationery	A one-year membership to the nicest gym in your area	Ten one-on-one Pilates sessions
$563	Transportation	A biweekly cleaning person so you can have your weekends back	This year's "in" boots
$1,739	Jewelry	A spur-of-the-moment weekend trip to [fill in the blank]	A laser treatment for your bikini area so you're always ready to bust out your two-piece
$922	Music	An airline ticket to go see Grandma, use the remainder on the therapy sessions you'll need afterward	Ditch Victoria's Secret and go La Perla all the way

"Club Wedd" advertising cuts to the chase with a couple kissing a blender below the headline "We Now Pronounce You Husband and Wife. You May Kiss the Gift." "What they really want" appears below the image. Aha! You knew it! They *are* in it for the gifts! But according to a survey conducted by The Knot, money is the most wanted item; only it's déclassé to ask for dough. So next time you visit your newlywed friend's home, why don't you suggest they break out that panini maker you gave them for their wedding? Betcha they returned it for cash.

- **if you were throwing the biggest party of your life?** Movies and television shows have been telling her for years that this is her big day, the most important day in her life. Even for those who know that a wedding is not literally the most important day of their lives, there's no question that it's still going to be the most expensive day. Seriously, who'd want the most expensive day of her life to suck? The logistics of planning a wedding can drain the life out of even the strongest, most down-to-earth women.

- **if you were making a million decisions that were being judged by your friends, Frenemies, and family?** "The wedding should really be a reflection of you and your fiancé," says the wedding planner, with dollar signs in her eyes. "It's a chance to express yourself." How are you going to show your friends and family your uniqueness? A remark from our friend the wedding photographer: "Brides always say they want their wedding to be different. I go to weddings for a living, and lemme tell you: They're. All. The. Same." But like it or not, the wedding is a statement. All eyes are on the bride, and when they aren't, they are looking around, making mental notes like "Cash bar, huh?" (Smirk.)

• **if you were given a gun and sent into the jungle with no guide?** The pressure to be creative extends to the registry. After all, the goods on this wish list represent how the couple plan on furnishing their life together. Are they kitschy country? Midcentury modern? Did she register at Saks and Barneys, leaving everyone to snicker about how presumptuous they are? Women who cook only when under duress are suddenly registering for top-of-the-line food processors and knives that seem suitable only for a samurai. Why? Imagine you're the bride-to-be and you spend ten minutes wandering around the housewares department, looking for the registry area, something you never knew existed before. Once you find it, you are lured into an office. (It's like entering some parallel universe. Who knew there were offices hidden in the walls of the housewares department?) A consultant will prattle on and on about the pros and cons of bed ruffles while you will realize with mounting anxiety that you have no idea what you want, how many of them you need, and how it's possible that you lived such a complete life up till now with nary a luxury damask sham in sight.

Registry consultant: Have you given much thought to your casual dining ware?

B2B (*staring blankly*): Excuse me?

Registry consultant (*forging ahead*): Have you considered chargers in lieu of place mats? Many brides are going this route these days.

B2B (*obviously clueless as to what a charger is*): A charger? Oh, of course . . . definitely.

G2B (*laughing*): I have a charger already, right, hon? She loves her Visa.

Approximately ten minutes of questions later . . .

Registry consultant (*realizing that you have no idea what the hell he is talking about and you're unlikely to go with the Waterford*): Here is a list of what people usually register for. Here's a scanner gun. Turn it in when you're done. Good-bye.

Every day affianced couples are let loose with a gun and no idea how to use it. They wander through housewares departments and megamarts shooting items at random or armed with a list of status quo "suggestions" for them to seek out. Some of the items on this list are rare and hitherto unheard of, yet the couple continues to fire away on the assumption that they'll know what to do with them once they say "I do."

What the hell is your friend going to do with an electric melon baller? Nothing. She is playing the role of "fiancée" and she's not going to let her guests in on the dirty little secret that she has *no idea* what she'll ever need half of this stuff for! Even if she has never seen anyone use a Crock-Pot, it is still part of the idea of "grown up" that lives in her mind. And since it's on the list, by God, she is going to have one!

• **if you were overwhelmed with helpful tips, unique ideas, and etiquette must-haves?** For years you've seen them on the racks in bookstores and grocery lines. Sure, there are the women who read bridal mags before they even go on date one, but most girls wait until they are engaged to purchase one of these tomes. The ring on her finger is her entrée into this brief time when it is acceptable to buy a bridal mag and not ask the cashier to brown-bag it so no one sees. Opening one of these glossies, she is suddenly overwhelmed by marital minutiae she never thought of, like the two-pager on how to address an invitation to a couple in which both people are doctors and have kept their last names.

• **if you were trying to please everyone at once?** The old idea that the bride's family foots the bill for the wedding is no longer a hard-and-fast rule. According to an online survey by The Knot, 37 percent of engaged couples stated that everyone involved (bride and groom, both sets of parents, sometimes grandparents) would be paying the bill, and 31 percent said that the engaged couple would be covering the costs themselves. Call it a case of too many cooks in the kitchen. Chipping in not only buys the limousine, it also buys an opinion as to whether it should be white stretch or Hummer.

- **if you were trying to avoid being the next Runaway Bride?** There was no way we could write a book about wedding pressure and not mention the real-life runaway bride, Jennifer Wilbanks, who was so freaked out about her four-hundred-plus-person wedding that she faked her own kidnapping just to avoid her big day. Your lobridemized friend may be trying to keep it all in check so that she doesn't pull a Jennifer at her own wedding.

- **if you were planning one day for seventeen months?** Can you think of anything else that's over in five hours that you plan for so long? The average length of engagement went from eleven months in 1990 to seventeen months in 2004.[3] We don't know about you, but that's a lot of time to second-, triple-, and quadruple-guess yourself before retreating into a paralysis of indecision. What bliss!

- **if you were vowing to be with someone till death do you part?** She's decided to spend the rest of her life with one person. As in the *same* person, day in, day out, for the next forty years or so. When you haven't even been alive that long, it's hard to get your head around doing something for four decades. It's easier to discuss the color of a shoe dye than think about the enormity of the commitment she's about to make. Focusing on the details may be her way of transferring the real stress of a major milestone in her life.

Believe It or Kn◯t

With this (2-carat, princess-cut, Tiffany-setting) ring I thee wed

Today a diamond ring is the ultimate symbol of the bride-to-be, a public display not only that someone picked you but also a sign of just how well you did. (Think we're kidding? One of our friends summed it up best: "I'd rather have no ring than a small one. That's just sad.") But a diamond ring wasn't always de rigueur—we can thank the fat cats on Madison Avenue for that. In the late 1800s, new diamond mines were discovered and the market value of the once-rare gem began to plummet. De Beers, which has a near monopoly of the diamond trade, sensed a fiscal crisis and sent a call to arms to its ad agency. The result: the award-winning 1939 "A diamond is forever" campaign, uniting the idea of finding true love with forking over (at least) two months' salary. Seventy-four percent of all brides now receive diamond engagement rings.

They're coming for you next! The folks at the Diamond Trading Company got wise and realized that they were missing a large market segment: women with disposable incomes and no fiancés. Thus, the "right-hand ring" was born. Let's analyze those ads: "Your left hand dreams of love. Your right hand makes dreams come true. Your left hand lives happily ever after. Your right hand lives happily here and now. Women of the world, raise your right hand." In other words, you're no desperate woman on the hunt for a rock. You're single and fine with it, thank you very much, and the thousand-dollar bauble you bought proves it. But if sisters are doing it for themselves, all right, we don't need to buy into the cult of the diamond to prove that we are independent and successful.

Is She at Risk? How to Know Your Friend May Have Had a Lobridemy

- Is she suddenly starting most of her sentences with the words "My wedding planner says . . ."?
- At a fitting, does she discuss with the tailor what size dress she should order based on her plan to go on a 1,200-calorie-a-day, Pilates-three-times-a-week regimen for the next six months?
- Has she mentioned a few times that she may take a leave of absence from her job to plan her wedding because "there are just too many things to do"?
- Have you stopped wanting to call her because you can't stand to hear any more about why pure white was the right choice over antique ivory?
- Has her former passion for after-hours skinny-dipping and environmental activism been supplanted by an equal excitement about something like place cards?

If you answered yes to any of these, chances are your friend is on the road to lobridemy-land. Her brain has been hijacked by hitching hysteria. Never fear. We have a few tactics for toughing it out that don't include moving to another state and meeting all new people.

Rx for the Lobridemized (and You, Too)

So what's a friend to do? Are you worried that one day you are going to blow a gasket in the middle of Bloomingdale's and blurt out that you couldn't care less about her wedding, honeymoon, dress, or registry? It doesn't have to come to that. Here are some roles you can play when dealing with your lobridemized friend.

The Kind Nurse

Kind Nurse listens with an open ear and offers heartfelt advice to her patients. If you choose this role, you will immerse yourself in her thought pattern, help her deliberate over whether or not to throw the bouquet, and hold her hand as she picks her table runners.

Pros
1. **Free food.** Who doesn't want to spend an afternoon tasting cakes and frostings?
2. **Seating power.** If you are a part of the planning, you can be sure that you will not be relegated to the loser table. Is

her cute cousin coming to the wedding? Might he like to sit next to your scintillating self?

3. **Dress veto.** You may not be able to tell the bride that you were thinking strapless when she's set on cap sleeves, but what if you volunteer to take some of the weight off of her by preselecting four or five different bridesmaid dress options for her to choose from? And if all the choices just happen to flatter your figure *and* fit into your budget, then so much the better!

4. **Payback.** After listening to the white-versus-ivory debate for a total of sixteen hours, you are guaranteed some sweet reciprocity. When it is your own turn to lose your mind over such inane details as which type of silk works best as a chair cover bow, you'll have someone who is absolutely indebted to you.

Cons

1. **Bodily harm.** You may be inclined toward self-inflicted violence for your martyrdom and to spare yourself further involvement. ("If I have to look at another bridal magazine, I'm going to poke my eyes out.")

2. **Inadequate recognition.** A main lobridemy symptom is absolute self-centeredness. If you're worried about getting your props, then Kind Nurse is not the best role for you.

3. **Bridesmaids' attack.** Sure, you love your bridesmaid dress, but if the other ladies know that you're to blame for the fuchsia knee-length dress that highlights your slim calves but leaves their cankles exposed to the crowd, then get ready to be blamed. The other bridesmaids may know not to bitch to the bride, but *you* are fair game.

Physical Therapist

With just a little tough love and some simple exercises, the Physical Therapist works on rehabilitating her lobridemized friend. You take her to places that have nothing to do with nuptials. You steer conversations away from color schemes and back to whether or not you should buy the boots you are trying on.

Pros
1. **Relief.** The patient will be glad to have a friend who gives her a respite from the stress of planning a wedding. Helping you with your problems will give her a much-needed break.
2. **Pink-slip peril.** You may save her from herself. Is your lobridemized friend also a co-worker? Remind her that your company monitors time spent online and that everyone walking by can tell she is working on her wedding binder and not her big presentation, which, by the way, is tomorrow.

Cons
1. **Missing a sensitivity chip.** *Doesn't she know that I am trying to plan a wedding?* You may seem less than sympathetic. After all, this is an important time in your friend's life, and here she is trying to share that with you and what do you do? Wrest the conversation right back to you. Who cares about your new, quite possibly psychotic boss?

36

2. **A losing battle.**
You: There was a fire in my apartment building last night, and I lost everything!
Her: Good thing your bridesmaid dress is at my house, safe and sound!

For some lobridemized women, all rehabilitation efforts are a waste of time.

The Escapist

One minute you're here, the next you're gone. When your friend's eyes zone out and the conversation turns to rectangular tables versus rounds, you make like a banana and split. You aren't free to help pick locations because you suddenly remembered that you promised to help your grandma with her garden. You fall ill just before dress shopping. You're out.

Pros
1. **No "I've had it up to here" rant.** You avoid the moment when you freak out on your friend, knock on her head, and say, "Hello, anyone home?" If you know yourself and know that you are not going to be a positive force in your friend's life, it may be best to make yourself scarce for a little while.
2. **A weekend to yourself.** You save yourself hours of soon-to-be-married misery. This alone may make it worth your while to Houdini yourself for a weekend or two. The lo-bridemized will never understand why you wouldn't want

to go searching for dyeable shoes with her, so just remove yourself from the situation completely. Go out of town or make like you have to work for the weekend. It's your right!

Cons

1. **Karma.** What if you end up being the annoying, boring bride-to-be one day? If you Houdini a friend, she just may Houdini you right back, and then you'll be stuck going to fittings with your MIL to-be, who likes to casually ask if you've ever given the Atkins Diet a try.
2. **Alienation.** Sure, you can bail on your friend-of-a-friend or your second cousin's errands, but when it comes to your girls, you have to suck it up and join in the discussions. If your disappearing act causes a rift in your friendship, it would be a real shame. It may seem easy to shift gears and focus on your single, nonlobridemized friends but one by one, they could just as easily leave you, too. If you think that your friendship will be harmed by your Houdini move, don't do it. You may even surprise yourself with how strongly you feel about buffet style being the wrong choice for her reception.

Understanding the beastly bridal biz can save a friendship—and possibly your own sanity down the line. You will get your friends back with a little effort sometime after the honeymoon, if you hold on. But make sure to get some space before their crazy-ass antics drive you nuts, too. You'll need to conserve your strength for the whole series of events you have coming up to celebrate the fact that everyone else is getting married but you. (Did they really think you'd forget?)

Repeat After Us

I promise to try to understand why my friend is constantly asking my opinion about everything from a DJ to the color of rose petals her flower girls are going to toss. I understand that she is certifiably insane from the perfect-day pressure, and that's exactly where the wedding industry wants her, so she keeps self-medicating by spending oodles of money. That does not mean that I will not take the necessary precautions to protect myself from being bored to tears by her monotonous wedding talk, and thank my lucky stars that I'm not in her shoes. When shopping for a friend's gift from her registry, I will get her the most arcane item that I can afford and then ask about it when I am visiting her home. I promise not to comment on any part of her wedding that could have gone better, unless of course she hurls an insensitive "We need to get you a man" or some such comment my way, because if that happens, all bets are off. And last, I will close my eyes and ears to all right-hand ring propaganda because I understand that it's a clever ploy to get me to spend a ton of dough masked in the cloak of feminism.

CHAPTER 3

Navigating Wedding Season

From deciphering the invite to dancing the macarena:
how to enjoy the fetes without racking up debts

You open your mailbox, and it's jammed. No, the September is-sues of *Vogue* and *InStyle* didn't arrive at the same time. Thick, creamy, odd-sized envelopes (which require extra postage to mail) tumble out with your credit card bills. You look at the envelopes and hardly recognize your own name due to the overdone calligraphy. It can mean only one thing—wedding invitations. Ah, wedding season, that period between June and October when the majority of the population gets hitched.[1] What does that mean for you, dear reader? Another money-sucking summer when every other weekend from Memorial Day to Labor Day you're booked in exotic places like Akron, Ohio, and Cos Cob, Connecticut.

Weddings celebrate the coming together of two people—winners in the game of love. And not only do we celebrate this union at the wedding, oh no, we have engagement parties, bridal showers, and bachelorette parties leading up to the main event, often followed by after-parties and next day brunches. And each celebration involves time, money, and forced Kodak

Believe It or Kn⬭t

Ever wonder why getting married in June is so popular? One legend kicking about has it that people took their yearly bath in May, which meant the betrothed couple would still smell good enough in June that neither bride nor groom would flee the altar holding their noses. But just in case they were starting to ripen, the bride carried a bouquet of flowers to hide any BO.[2] Lovely.

moments. Lily, thirty-three, upbeat and single, told us she sees weddings "as happy and optimistic. I mean, they sure beat all the family funerals I've been to." Way to be positive, Lily. Then again, she wasn't talking about having to pin the tail on the penis at a bachelorette blowout. Not all of us take such a positive view on these dough-draining affairs. That thick white envelope is your ticket to the wonderful world of nuptial nonsense. Now, don't toss the envelope away because the handwritten calligraphy or expensive typesetting on the front is an important clue to the labyrinth of etiquette you will soon be negotiating—one that makes the lines at the DMV look like a straight shot.

- If there is an envelope in an envelope, get ready for a fancy affair.
- Was the envelope hand-addressed, or is the couple going with the DIY home-label-printing technique? DIY indicates

a money-conscious couple and probably a more relaxed affair overall.

- A hand stamp means that the sender schlepped to the post office and requested hand stamps for the invitations. This kind of attention to detail will probably play out through to the out-of-town gift baskets.

- No RSVP card? That means that the bride has read up on etiquette and expects guests to send individual replies.

- Does it say "and guest"? Well, lucky you—at least you can bring someone and not have to sit at the singles table with the bride's teenage cousins.

- Is the registry mentioned anywhere inside that envelope? Mentioning the registry is a major faux pas. Get ready for more etiquette missteps. Keeping track of them can become a whole game of its own.

Believe It or Kn⬭t

One B2B queried a friend about including a bank routing number *on the invitation* so guests could "conveniently" direct deposit money into her account. When Janet, twenty-seven, emphatically tried to convince her that this would be beyond tacky, the B2B staunchly defended her idea. Her logic: "We already live together and have everything we need. All we want is money." As we go to press, Janet has yet to see the invitations.

Sound like your own private hell? Not to worry—we'll get you through these functions with cash in your wallet, a smile on your face, and a modicum of dignity.

The Engagement Party: The Fun Has Just Begun

Traditionally, the bride's family hosted an engagement party to formally announce the couple's plans to marry. Today, however, after you've gotten the mass "we're engaged" e-mail or IGBN call, the engagement party isn't exactly breaking news. Still, it's a good sneak peek at the crowd you'll be boogying with come wedding time. Some engagement party FAQs:

- **Do I need to bring a present?** No, a gift is not required, and the couple shouldn't be opening anything they do receive during the party. (Read: You don't have to worry that you'll be outed as a cheapskate.) That said, it's increasingly common to bring a token present. Here are three ideas that say class without breaking the bank:

  1. A bottle of bubbly, or even sparkling wine, is always appropriate for the celebration. Just keep in mind that you don't have to drop a C-note on Veuve Clicquot La Grande Dame. There are plenty of lesser-known champagnes and sparkling wines that are just as good as the primo names you hear in hip-hop songs. Also, getting a bottle that is not a brand name will make it look as though you know about wines. If you aren't exactly an oenophile or have no idea what oenophile means, go to

a local wine store, tell the clerk what the occasion is and about how much you want to spend, and get a recommendation. Don't worry about sounding cheap. When it comes to vino, more money doesn't always mean better juice. If you don't have access to a friendly wine shop, check out Wine.com for sparkling wine and champagne recommendations at every price. Stuck without the Internet? Our recs for three top-rated bottles of sparkling wine that won't send you to the poorhouse:

- Dom. Chandon Etoile, Napa Valley, California: $29.99
- Canella NV Prosecco di Conegliano, Veneto, Italy: $19.99
- Cristalino NV Brut Cava, Spain: $8.99

2. Find a frame and insert your favorite photo of the happy couple. Remember, not only do people love to talk about themselves, they also love to look at themselves! We've found great frames at: T.J. Maxx, Marshalls, Ross, and the local drugstore.

3. Head to a nursery—or even your local mega–food store. Buy a small potted plant, something hearty that won't die easily, like a cyclamen or a begonia. When you give your gift to the betrothed, see if you can say— without gagging—that you hope this plant blooms through the years as you know their love will. If you can get through that with a straight face, give yourself major points. Plus, your host will think you're oh-so-

considerate for not bringing cut flowers and forcing her to dig through her cabinets in search of a vase while she's trying to make sure no one spills coffee on her new white couch.

If you can't attend the party, or you are not bringing a gift, take the time to buy a card or whip out your nice stationery, and write the couple a note of congratulations.

Handwritten letters are less and less common, so this small gesture will seem very considerate and classy. We recommend having plain stationery in a thick stock on hand at all times. Not only will it save you from rushing out and blowing $6 on a specific-occasion card, but it's always elegant for anything from a thank-you note to a condolence card.

- **Can I bring a date?** Not if you aren't invited with a guest or a plus one. Typically, the only people at an engagement party are the ones getting invitations to the big-top event. So if you're flying solo, smile and scope the crowd to find a potential ally. You'll need one.

- **The wedding season PIC (partner-in-crime).** Chances are, everyone who attends the engagement party will be in attendance at all the events, so don't waste the opportunity. Survey the party for another single woman who looks as if she is having as much fun as you are. Saunter over and introduce yourself. If she seems like someone you could hang with, come right out and ask if she would like to be your wedding buddy. Having the right wedding buddy can turn a drab time into a night to remember.

Wedding buddy duties include:

- Sharing knowing *gag-me* looks as the B2B opens boring gift after boring gift at the bridal shower
- Coming to the rescue at the reception when either of you is cornered by the bride's touchy-feely uncle
- Getting onto the dance floor when the electric slide comes on (because you have to let loose and dance at least a little)
- Making fun of the other guests
- Vetting any hookups for blood relations
- Making sure you both get home safely

The Bridal Shower: The Longest Three Hours on a Saturday You'll Never Get Back

The typical shower is a women-only event, so welcome to estrogen purgatory. Here is where the gaggle of hens will cluck about why you aren't married, interrogate you about who you're dating, and tell you you need to wear a skirt more often. The B2B will get up and start opening her gifts, usually assisted by her ladies in waiting, who hand over the packages and help record who gave what. Our advice for this absurd affair: If you can't beat 'em, join 'em! As in, go full-on Stepford. Put on your girliest getup and pretend you are an extra in a Douglas Sirk weepie. Do your best Doris Day, and you will get through everything from the gifts to the games with a smile on your face. It may be the frozen smile of a be-Valiumed fifties housewife, but hey, it's better than a scowl.

Believe It or Kn⬭t

The couple already had their engagement party, they are just about to have their bachelor/bachelorette parties, what does she need a bridal shower for? The origin of this seemingly gratuitous gift-giving affair dates back to a Dutch folktale in which the daughter of a rich man wanted to marry a poor miller. Her father disapproved, so he refused to provide the dowry. The townspeople felt sorry for the couple, so they showered them with gifts to help her set up house.[3] Bet you didn't think that you were part of providing a dowry for your found-true-love-and-now-we're-a-dual-income-household friend.

Getting Through the Games: How to Go for the Gold or at Least Not Forfeit Completely

What games? you ask. If you have yet to encounter one of these time fillers, you've been pretty damn lucky.

- **The Clothespin Game.** When you enter the party, you are given a clothespin to wear somewhere visible. The rules vary slightly but usually go like this: a particular buzzword like "bride" or "wedding" is off limits, or maybe those zany shower ladies have decided you can't cross your legs. Whatever the forbidden word or action, if you see someone say or do it, you get to take her clothespin. The woman with the most clothespins at the end of the shower gets the prize. Lame? Heck, yes. However, for us competitive ladies it does provide a nice focus for when you think you may hurl if you hear another giggle come out of your formerly sarcastic friend who turned into one of "them" the moment she slipped the diamond on her finger.

- **Bridal Trivia.** This game could also be called "I know her better than you do." The organizer of the party puts together a quiz about the bride, her fiancé, and their engagement. You could have fun with this game by shouting out very wrong but bitingly funny answers. As in "You mean the time Rachel did Jell-O shots and made out with that fat guy?" If you do it in a lighthearted way, you could be seen as the hilarious "why hasn't anyone scooped her up yet?" girl. This is a tightrope move, however, since one comment too many (or a poorly receptive audience), and you could just as easily be the "had too much to drink and trying to steal attention from the bride" girl.

The best part of these games? The fact that there are winners. And um, prizes. When was the last time you left a party with a goody bag? If you are *in* enough with the organizer, volunteer to pick out the booty so that you will know which bag to pick when you take home the blue ribbon. Our picks for prizes if you're the bag maker: think fun, lighthearted gifts that won't offend anyone invited to the soiree. In other words, no how-to-have-hotter-sex gift books. Some safe ideas that always make girls happy:

- **Dessert.** This theme could include all things yummy like a vanilla candle, fancy chocolates, strawberry lip gloss.

- **Bed, bath, and beyond.** This bag could contain bubble bath, room spray, and an eye mask or bath pillow.

- **Coffee, tea, and thee.** This one is easy: buy a bag of whole coffee beans, a box of fancy loose tea, and a tea diffuser. If you really want to go for it, include a mug.

- **Regift bag.** Have you received a completely random gift from someone guaranteed *not* to be in attendance? Volunteer it for a bag. A friend did this with a fancy chopsticks set.

- **Wine lover.** A semidecent bottle of wine, a set of cute wineglass charms, and a vacuum sealer to keep the wine from turning if she doesn't polish it off in one sitting. Easy one-stop shopping at a place like BevMo! or Total Beverage.

The Jack 'n' Jill Shower

Billed by some to be "progressive," we smart ladies know better. The couples shower is really just an excuse for the guy to get presents, too. The good news? If you have a boyfriend, he has to endure the party with you. The bad news? You both lose a perfectly good Saturday fielding questions like "So, are you two next?"

Etiquette Rules for Shower Gifts

If the couple has registered for their wedding gifts, it is a safe bet to buy her a gift from her registry. Sometimes these functions even have themes, like time of day and seasons of the year. Nope, we're not kidding. If you are invited to a time-of-day party, your invitation will include a specific time, and the gift you buy should make sense for that time. Say you are given morning, then give a gift she can use in the morning. These theme parties, while seemingly cheesy, are actually a great way to get around the registry (and the bride knowing how much you spent!).

Get creative with these types of presents:

Theme: Time of Day

Morning	Afternoon	Night
A coffee-of-the-month subscription for your java-addicted friend	Travel guide geared toward short road trips, perfect for a mellow afternoon	A poker set for her own casino night—don't forget a CD of *The Gambler* by Kenny Rogers
A weekend subscription to the local newspaper	Tickets to an aquarium, botanical garden, or national park	Tickets to an upcoming play

Theme: Seasons of the Year

Spring	Summer	Fall	Winter
Some gardening tools and seeds to get her garden growing	A picnic basket; food enjoyed outdoors is always a good time	Are they into sports? Nothing says fall like tickets to a local college football game	A membership to your local museum will keep her out of the cold and usually comes with perks, plus you'll flatter her sense of sophistication

A WORD OF WARNING IF YOU HAVE TO THROW ONE OF THESE PARTIES

Josie's friend asked her if she wanted a theme for her bridal shower. Josie had no idea what she was talking about, so when her friend suggested a boudoir party, Josie figured "Why not?" Sounded like she'd get stuff she'd normally never get for herself: girly, lacy things, overpriced bath products, and luxurious sheets. Other people had a slightly different interpretation: at the shower, Josie's future mother-in-law not only watched as Josie opened racy item after racy item but also proceeded to give Josie the raunchiest bra and underwear set herself. Total Frederick's of Hollywood. Josie was not sure what was worse, that her future mother-in-law thought she would like the set or the insight into her MIL's sex life and bedroom fashion style. Josie cursed herself for not doing a "seasons of the year" theme instead.

We ♥ Google

Enter "bridal shower planning," and you'll be shocked at how many sites are dedicated to the art of the shower. Some common themes:

- **Stock the pantry.** Guests write a favorite recipe on a card and bring it, along with all nonperishable ingredients she'll need for the recipe. If your crowd is from the "throw the Lean Cuisine in the microwave and press start" school of cooking, you might want to broaden it to a "favorites" theme and have guests bring their favorite hand cream, cocktail mix, TV show on DVD, candles. . . .

- **Entertaining.** Just bring something that has recreation written all over it: puzzles, board games, badminton set, bocce balls, Frisbee, karaoke machine.

- **Books.** Everyone selects a book they think will be useful in married life. (What not to bring: *The Woman's Book of Di-*

vorce: 101 Ways to Make Him Suffer Forever and Ever). Or you could even jump the gun and get a book on child rearing. Way to kiss up to the MIL and MOB!

• **Spa.** A no-brainer: this theme would include gifts like manicure sets, massage oil, facial masks, spa gift certificates, and plush robes.

Whether you're going to a themed event or a standard shower, the bottom line is, it's her party, and you need to bring a gift if you want to come.

The Bachelorette Party: Girls Gone Wild

One last hoorah for her, another reminder of how much it sucks to be single for you. Bachelorette parties are the exact opposite of the bridal shower. Instead of being on her best behavior, all of a sudden your affianced friend is wearing a "suck for a buck" T-shirt and doing blowjob shots at a skanky club. What's a right-minded friend to do?

Preparing for her big night out: Depending on your mood, attitude, and proximity to the planning of this affair, you can play it one of two ways. You can be the sober voice of reason that ensures that your friend will remember her party. Duties include things like ordering a glass of water for every Sex on the Beach drink someone buys the B2B. Or, if you have the stomach for it, you can be the one to get this party started, right. Be the bachelorette ringleader. Sometimes it's easier to throw yourself into a scenario rather than try to distance yourself from it.

This will make you the life of the party *and* be a nice bit of revenge for that four-hour shower you had to suffer through, not to mention the $200 you just dropped on a nice puce number with puffy sleeves.

Throw the best bachelorette party she'll never remember.

1. Go to your local "adults only" store with your crew and get penis everything: penis straws that glow in the dark, a penis hat, even a penis cake (you can order from a specialized shop, like The Erotic Bakery, but it's much cheaper to buy a mold and make your own. We like to use a pound cake recipe). Too shy or your town has laws against these kinds of stores? Online sites that can help you locate just the right accoutrements for your party: BacheloretteParties.com and bachelorettepartyfun.com.

2. Get together with a couple of other women to devise a list of things that the B2B must accomplish before the night is over. Things like getting a guy to kiss her feet, dancing up on the bar, or performing the macarena are always appropriate.

3. Set up a preparty. Prior to hitting the clubs, plan to meet up at someone's home for the preparty festivities. Get games like Pin the Penis on the Pin-Up or Penis Piñata and let the good times begin. Each attendee should bring a sexy gift and watch the B2B open them in horror as she realizes what is in store for her.

4. Pick an appropriate venue. If you are going to help throw a bachelorette party, go all the way. No chic restaurant or bar. Head to a loud, ridiculous dance club. There are definite bachelorette destinations. You'll know you're in the

right place if you see at least three other B2Bs wearing veils with condoms glued on them.

5. Keep it PG-13. Laughing at her shaking her booty to Kanye is a good time, letting her get falling-down drunk or make out with some random guy is not a good time. Exact a little revenge, but don't jeopardize her relationship or safety. You are still her friend, and you should take it easy on the booze yourself so that not only will you remember all of her antics, but also you will be able to play referee and call the night when it's over.

Once the booze starts flowing, so does your cash. Here are three ways to party the night away without a financial hangover:

1. Order for the table. If your party starts with a dinner out, delegate one person to order food for the table. You'll keep costs down by splitting a number of apps, salads, and entrées instead of each person ordering her own app, salad, and entrée. Restaurant serving sizes are too big anyway, and it's hard to shake your thang when you're stuffed.

2. You are not a VIP. Clubs are quick to offer a VIP table, but beware, to many clubs this just means paying by the bottle (and out the ear)! Recently, someone told us she ended up paying $300 for a bottle of bottom-shelf vodka!

3. Why go out? If someone has a big enough place, make the dinner a potluck, stock up the bar, play the games, and have the stripper come to you. You'll save tons of dough. Be sure to volunteer to come back the next day to help clean up the inevitable mess. Even better, bring a sleeping

bag and turn the party into a slumber party. The best part of that idea? No drinking-and-driving concerns!

HINT

Leave the Camera at Home

Ever notice that you never see pictures of a bachelor party, yet at least four women will bring their cameras to a bachelorette? Men know not to have any embarrassing evidence. The bachelorette should be a secret woman thing. What happens there should stay there.

Always the Bridesmaid . . . Always an Ugly Dress

The last time another woman picked out your outfit, you were seven and wore Hush Puppies. Even if your frock isn't fugly (depending on your comfort level with the F-word, that either means fantastically ugly or f***ing ugly), the reality is that you are not going to wear it again, ever. So remember when you agree to stand up for your friend at the altar: You buy whatever dress she tells you to, whether it's ridiculously priced or in a color that makes you look jaundiced. And yep, you pay for it. Including any fittings. And dyeable shoes, if that's what she wants. Really, it's enough to make you want to get married just for payback.

While you may never wear that dress again, you have some options:

- **eBay it.** Remember, one woman's mauve nightmare is another woman's dream dress! If you are friends with the other bridesmaids you can all put your dresses up for auction at the same time, or sell them as a group to some other unfortunate souls.

- **Donate your dress to charity.** Warm the cockles of your heart knowing your dress has gone on to a more noble cause. Cinderellaproject.org provides donated formal dresses to underprivileged teenage girls for things like Prom. Bonus: you'll get receipts you can use for a tax time deduction.

- **Pretty in Pink it.** If you've got a good tailor and it's worth putting in some money, see if he or she can alter it into something wearable. For example, a floor-length satin dress can be converted into a cocktail dress by taking off a few inches and making it tea (or knee) length.

Believe It or Kn☺t

There *are* dresses uglier than yours. Check out uglydress.com for some really heinous frocks or browse the coffee table book *You Can Wear it Again: A Celebration of Bridesmaid Dresses* by Meg Mateo Ilasco. Really, yours could have been worse.

The Big Day: You're Almost There . . . Just One More Party to Get Through

The wedding itself is a minefield of etiquette. How do you decline an invitation without looking like a jerk? Can you bring your new boyfriend? How about your roommate? Does an evening wedding necessarily mean black tie? Are you going to be stuck at a crappy table? Is your boyfriend even worthy of being your +1? Relax, and listen up.

RSVP Etiquette

About seven weeks before the actual wedding, you will receive your invitation in the mail. You have an important choice to make at this point: Are you in or are you out?

- **Just say no.** If this is your eleventh invitation of the year and your heart sinks at the thought of going, or if the timing coincides with your much-beloved annual family reunion, or you simply just don't want to go, then check the "regretfully decline" box. It's your only chance to bail on going to the wedding. Some things that may help you decide: Is your absence going to be noticeable? Will it harm your friendship? If so, you may have to suck it up. When declining, include a little note that lets them know how upset you are to miss the happy occasion and wish them a lovely day. And yes, even if you don't attend the wedding you should send a gift.

- **Reply quickly.** No one will ever cop to this, but there's going to be an A-list and a B-list. The A-list consists of people the couple definitely wanted to invite. Then, based on the number of "regrets," they move on to their B-list. If you know you cannot attend, let the couple know as soon as you do so they can move on.

- **Managing multiple invites.** Say you've got three different invites for Labor Day (brides love to think that there's no better way you'd want to spend a holiday weekend than at their wedding). Your little trick to deciding who makes the cut? Obviously the first rule should be your relationship to the person. If you were getting married, would it really mean a lot if this person was there? The second rule should be reverse strategy: if you got the invite about three weeks before the actual date, face it: You're a C-lister to her, so why bother stressing about showing up?

- **They mean what they say.** If the invitation does not say "and guest," it means that you have to go on your own. If the invitation says your name and the name of a guy whom you are no longer seeing, you cannot bring whomever you happen to be seeing at the time. Couples take time with the phrasing of these invitations.

A true story: Julia was planning a very small wedding and wanted only people she knew to attend. She decided that if her friends were not in a serious relationship, they couldn't bring a guest. She was shocked to see that her friend Catherine, who had just had her first date with a new guy, had written in "and guest" on her RSVP. Julia called her to explain that she couldn't bring anyone because they were trying to keep their wedding intimate. Catherine became indignant and told Julia that she wouldn't go if she couldn't bring her date. Julia stuck to her guns, Catherine didn't attend the wedding, and they haven't really spoken since. Don't forget what we taught you in Chapter 2: You can't mess with a woman on the verge of a lobridemy. It's a solo show or a no-go. Period.

What If the Wedding Is in Croatia?

Have you been invited to one of these yet? Destination weddings can be many things (tacky, expensive), but they tend not to be the vacation of your dreams.

Do You Have to Go? How to Be There for a Pal Without Draining Your Savings Account

By planning a destination wedding, the couple is signing up for a lot of "regretfully declines." These are the easiest weddings to say no to. That said, you still have to send a gift. If you think that their plan is to get as many gifts as possible with as few attending guests as possible, you can always make a charitable donation in their name and send them a card letting them know what you have done. No present for them; no wedding for you. Score one for charity.

If you do decide to go, hold your complaining in check. Or

at least reserve the commentary about how inconvenient these outlandish nuptials are for the wedding buddy you are about to partner up with. Travel expenses can be cut by finding a similarly single invitee to share a hotel, rental car, and even gas. If you are our kind of frugal, you can even split dinner along the way. Another thing: You don't *have* to stay in the fancy hotel the bride and groom recommend for their guests. There's always a light on at Motel 6.

If you know your travel buddy, consider turning the trip into a real vacation. If you're already flying to Saint Thomas, why hurry home? Stay an extra week and have an adventure. The airfare is likely to be a significant cost of the trip, so once you have shelled out that cash it makes sense to get as much bang for your buck as possible.

Okay, I'm Going, Now What Should I Wear?

People are way too camera-happy at weddings to risk a sartorial slip-up. Follow these guidelines so people remember you, not your fashion faux pas.

• While wearing black is generally more acceptable nowadays, even for a daytime affair, think flowery, not funereal. In other words, a black sundress with white flowers? Okay. A black suit with hat? Not so much. It's pretty much fair game after that with One. Major. Exception: Don't wear white.

• You'll also want to look seasonally and temporally appropriate, if for no other reason than the comfort factor.

There's nothing worse than going to a May wedding in a sundress when it's 40 degrees and pouring outside.

- Morning and afternoon services are generally more casual than evening affairs.

- When they say black tie, they mean it. Bust out the sequins and sparkle if that's your thing. Traditionally, this also meant floor-length for women, but these days there's not a hard-and-fast rule. Just think of it as fancy. If your date is not thrilled about renting a tux, a black suit with a dark tie should blend in just fine.

- If a wedding is described as casual, ask around to see what other people are wearing. You don't want to show up in a sundress and heeled sandals when everyone else is in shorts or bathing suits. Sonya learned the hard way: "Why didn't they say it was a pool party?" she remarked after spending the day trying to keep her heels from sinking into the grass at the backyard reception.

Looking Good Without Going Broke

If you're cash-strapped because you've got a major tour of duty (six weddings in four months), try to think ahead and see if you can find one dress that could work for almost all, by changing wraps, shoes, purses, and jewelry. It's usually easiest to do this with a simple dress. Lillian, for example, once found a strapless black dress with an asymmetrical hem in the junior department at Nordstrom. It cost about $50 and with different accessories and layering, worked for a variety of weddings (and some other events) over a two-year stretch. You'd be surprised at what you can find by hitting the juniors' racks, at a fraction of the price for something similar one floor up. Other spots for great deals:

- Discount stores: Ross, T.J. Maxx, Filene's Basement, Loehmann's, Marshalls
- Online retailers: Girlshop.com (the sale area), Bluefly.com
- A similarly sized friend's closet

When Should I Get There?

If an invitation says that the ceremony starts at 4:00, be in your seat at 3:50. If you are running late for some reason, skip the ceremony and keep the fact that you skipped it to yourself. Don't tell the couple how bummed you are that you missed the actual tying of the knot. In this case, what they don't know won't hurt them.

Don't Let Your Inner Drunk Girl Out

An open bar + your Aunt Ethel's love advice + seeing your ex with his fab new girlfriend = you potentially getting a bit too tipsy and making an ass of yourself. Nobody wants to be *that girl* who gets sloppy drunk and makes a scene. Best to have a plan. Go back to your college days and remember some basic rules:

- **Never mix your drinks.** Don't just drink whatever is handed to you. Patty told us about an Armenian wedding she attended where each table had bottles of hard liquor on it. Not only was there no drinking downtime while you waited for a bartender or waiter, but people were making their own concoctions and having the rest of the table try it. She has a vague recollection of a crew of roaming videographers and singing a rousing "Bridge over Troubled Water," but thankfully she has never had to watch the video.

- **Beware the bubbly.** Champagne is a fun drink and is definitely a necessity at a wedding. It is also the cause of many a wicked hangover. Sip it.

- **Alternate with H$_2$O.** For every glass of wine you have, have a glass of water. You will be hard pressed to get sloppy drunk with all of those trips to the bathroom.

- **Eat dinner.** At a very posh wedding Lori saw her boss learn this lesson. He was pretty far gone after the cocktail hour and then refused to eat dinner. Later on in the evening he also refused to stop smoking his obnoxious cigar on the dance floor. Security let him off with a warning, but he wasn't cut off from the bar. Big mistake. He accidentally dropped the maid of honor middip, laughed when she flashed the room her undies trying to get up, and continued to shake it like a Polaroid picture long after most of the guests had called it a night.

- **Arrange for a ride home.** Carpool with a pregnant friend or someone else who plans on staying sober for the evening.

Believe It or Kn⬭t

Half empty, half full, or just half off?
One of the many costly decisions a couple must make is how high to fill everyone's champagne glass for the wedding toast. If your glass is half full, someone was saving a few bucks.

- **Get into the groove:** *You* are in control of how much fun you have. Yes, people are going to ask you some potentially rude questions and there is going to be a lot of talk about love and luck and "meant to be." Mentally prepare yourself for this, and be ready to go on autopilot. If you can manage your own expectations for the night, you may surprise yourself and have a better time than you anticipated.

- **Look hot:** Another way to get psyched up for the big game? If you have the cash, get a manicure, have your eyebrows done, buy a new lipstick—whatever makes you feel good about yourself. Or don't spend a dime and just do an extra-long workout, or pamper yourself while you're getting ready. Take a long bath. Shave past your knees. When you feel good about how you look, you radiate a confidence that others will pick up on. And when it comes to getting your photo taken, remember: stand tall, shoulders down, and angle on your best side.

Getting Your Groove On at the Reception (and We Don't Mean the Conga Line)

Guys have always known this: It's pretty easy to score at a wedding. Why? Single girls are drowning in the Bridal Wave, so they'll cling to anything that'll keep 'em from going under. After you read this book, of course, you're going to be calm, cool, and totally treading. But if you feel up for some action, you can take your pick (especially if you took our advice and look hot).

While getting caught with the "help" can be humiliating, it beats hooking up with another guest, only to find out later that you're distantly related. Ew! Some prime targets: the bartender or any member of the band. And of course, the groomsmen are always game. One enterprising woman told us she seduced the photographer, which was fine—except that he ended up taking loads of pictures of her, and not so many of the bride. **A word of caution: Take your antics off the premises.** Make plans to meet up later or catch a ride after the reception ends. Don't get busted in the bathroom and cause somebody's grandma to have a coronary. Monica once attended a wedding where the MOB found the best man in the coat closet with the waitress. Getting caught with your skirt up while family members are around is not so cool.

In our survey, 45 percent of women claimed to have done some inappropriate dirty dancing at a wedding reception. Keep your stripperific routine to your pole-dancing class at the gym. You aren't an extra in a Britney video. Subtlety is key.

Surviving a Wedding When You've Got a Man but No Ring

A wedding can be the make-it-or-break-it point for both fledgling and veteran relationships. Kate and Nelson were together for seven years, and she felt like she was losing the race because all their friends were getting married and they weren't even engaged. "We'd go to weddings and I'd be like 'What's wrong with us that we're not up there? We're just as good—if not better—a couple.' It was even tougher to be at weddings for friends who had dated for less time than we have!" We told you not to compare and contrast. That + free booze + questions about when you two are going to get married = a recipe for disaster. If her wedding has you feeling bad about your own relationship and you need to get some things off your chest, by all means do so, just not when you are in a room full of your friends and their families.

From Erin
I was a maid of honor for my childhood friend and found out the day before her ceremony that my boyfriend was cheating on me. Since I had to partake

in all the wedding activities, I didn't see him until after the ceremony. I was so irate when I walked down the aisle that I nearly threw my bouquet at his head. When I met him at our table, I couldn't take sitting near him. He followed me into a back room, and we essentially missed the entire reception. He even had the gall to say, "I think you're blowing it out of proportion because you're seeing your friend make this lifelong commitment, and we're having problems." Ladies, I was furious because the creep was pursuing other (barely legal) women online, and I somehow didn't know this for two years! When I said good-bye to the bride's mother she must have thought I was tear-streaked from seeing my oldest friend tie the knot. She even said to me, "I love your boyfriend! You're going to be next, I bet." I bit the insides of my cheeks and grimaced, all the while fighting the urge to scream, "He's a worthless, lying loser!"

Avoiding Relationship Drama at a Wedding

The number one way to avoid conflict: dance. The number one way to guarantee drama: having a State of (Your) Union.

Why you should be a dancing machine:

- Less time at the table fielding "Are you two next?" questions
- Less time for you to wonder if his complimenting the filet

really means that he's thinking of his future wedding—to you!

- More time to metabolize champagne cocktails

Remember, the guy you bring to the wedding does not have to be the guy you marry.

Ka-ching! The Wedding May be Over, but the Spending Ain't

It used to be that you had up to a year to buy the couple a gift after the wedding (this was especially tempting for suspected starter marriages), but modern etiquette (um, online shopping) has speeded things up considerably. Give it three months, tops. The National Association of Wedding Ministers says that Americans spend approximately *$19 billion* annually on presents through gift registries. Just how much are you (or you and your date) expected to shell out when it comes to buying the wedding gift?

- Co-worker and/or a distant family friend or relative: $50–$75
- Relative or friend: $75–$100
- Close relative or close friend: $100–$150+[4]

And no, these don't include shipping or tax. No wonder you're dropping dough like there's no tomorrow. If you've got ten weddings in a year, you're looking at a minimum of $1,000 between the shower and wedding gifts, not counting travel and lodging! Now, we know there's nothing more stressful than feeling like you're the only one in your friendship circle who isn't in line for the altar and you're literally paying for it. And there's more bad news: don't shoot the messengers, but the rule of thumb is that you should never spend less than $50. Despite this unspoken law of loot, don't get hung up on the price as an indication of your friendship. In the end, a real friend is going to care only that you were there to share her day, not whether or not you bought her a Le Creuset casserole dish. If you do suspect she might be including you in her head count for your gift-giving potential, you might want to rethink the relationship.

Gift Ideas for the Credit-Challenged

Screw the registry!

- **Make a DVD.** You'll look like their most creative (and thoughtful) friend by scanning a bunch of photos, setting them to some music, adding a few titles ("But it was Jason's karaoke rendition of 'Total Eclipse of the Heart' that really cinched it for Rebecca . . ."), and using a little something called the "Ken Burns effect" to make the whole thing *über*-professional. Technically ambitious or want to get in touch with your inner Sofia Coppola? If you have a video camera, go ahead and make a wedding movie. Action!

- **Make a memory book.** If you've been friends with the couple for a while, gather photos of the evolution of their relationship and mount them in a photo album, leaving a few pages blank with a note that you hope they will fill it with more precious memories in their new life as a married unit. *Aw.*

- **Hit the outlets.** Grab a girlfriend and head to the outlet mall, where there are some amazing deals to be had. With big names like Williams-Sonoma, Le Creuset, Crate and Barrel, Polo Ralph Lauren, Pottery Barn, and Barneys offering outlet options, you're sure to find something wedding-appropriate. Once you find something you like, say, silver candleholders or an elegant serving tray, *buy in bulk.* Choose items that most people would like and avoid anything that screams, "This was bought at a day-after-Christmas sale!" Of course, while you're at the outlets, you may as well look for yourself. After all, you deserve a present, too.

- **She's crafty.** Use your skills, ladies! By donating your time and talent, you can do a variety of things that will cost you only the price of the materials. For example, crocheting an afghan (one friend we know has a gorgeous, one-of-a-kind piece that beats a Wamsutta throw any day) or building a bookcase or a bench for their porch. Another friend designed the wedding brochures, and another did the bride's hair and makeup. Yet another wrote a song for the happy couple, burned a CD, and framed the lyrics.

- **Get cookin'.** Are you a gourmet chef in the making? Gather your best recipes, create a customized cookbook, and put it in a basket with the basics she can't do without (extra-virgin olive oil, spices, etc.).

- **Safety in numbers.** If she's a close pal but spending more than $50 will break the bank (and be woefully obvious when you get her the $49.99 blender on her list), go in on a big-ticket item with a group of people. Chances are your friend is not going to do the math to see how much you all chipped in; she's just going to be psyched that someone ponied up to get that $700 espresso machine she *had* to have.

Sanity-Saving Vows

Repeat After Us

I promise to reply to all the invitations I get in a timely fashion and will occasionally say "no." I will cherish my own time and make sure I devote one weekend in a busy wedding season to myself. When I feel like I may blow my stack at a shower, I will sit back and make a game out of the event. I will try to anticipate whether the B2B will go "Ooh" or "Ahh" or say "I love it" with every gift opening. I will not go into credit card debt by thinking I have to buy fab new dresses and sex-me-up stilettos for every wedding I go to. I repeat, I will not go into credit card debt. I will love and honor my bridesmaid dress until the reception ends, and then it's death we do part in whatever way I choose. I recognize that someone else's wedding is a fabulous place to shake my groove thang, not to have a relationship check-in with my date. If I get busy with another guest (or the bread waiter), I will not take the dis-

posable camera to document it as revenge on the bride's "perfect" day. I will watch my own drinking by alternating alcohol with water, so as to protect myself from champagne goggles that might otherwise convince me that I never noticed the underage son of my parents' friends looks "just like" a young Johnny Depp. I will scout out a wedding buddy as early in the process as possible. Aside from having a partner in crime for the reception, I just may find that I have a new, similarly single friend.

CHAPTER 4

The Timeline

"I always thought I'd be married—or at least engaged—by now!" Why sticking to the script leads to bad decisions

After graduating from high school Amy went to her first-choice college, where she excelled in both academics and love. She had a string of great boyfriends, each of whom she broke up with before they got too serious because she wanted to experience life before settling down, which Amy thought would be around the age of twenty-six or twenty-seven, after she made some headway in her career. She moved to New York City after graduation and found an affordable apartment, which she shared with a fun, sassy girl named Tanya. Together they painted the town red. When she wasn't going out and having the time of her life, Amy was being lauded for her work at a prestigious firm. Just after turning twenty-four, she met Max. He was everything she had ever dreamed of—smart, sophisticated, from a good family, and her best friend. For her twenty-sixth birthday, he surprised her with a trip to St. Barts. During a moonlit walk on the beach Max dropped to one knee and asked Amy if she would make him the happiest man in the world. He opened a small black box containing the most beautiful two-carat, emerald-cut diamond ring from Tiffany & Co., *exactly* the ring that Amy would have picked out for herself. After a gorgeous wedding at his parents' house in Napa and a romantic honeymoon in Florence, Amy came back to one last surprise: he had bought a brownstone for them to start their life together in. And they lived happily ever after until . . .

Beep! Beep! Beep! Amy's alarm clock wakes her up. She hits the snooze button and tries to will herself back into her dream, but it's too late. As she drags herself out of bed (she can get out on only one side because the room is so cramped), she remembers that her boyfriend dumped her last week because he "felt like he would never be enough" for her—oh, and he had met someone else. She gets ready for her crappy admin job and curses herself for majoring in liberal arts at a second-tier school.

We all have secret designs for how our lives are supposed to go, but when has life ever gone according to plan? Despite our BlackBerrys and obsessive calendaring, we can control only things like our credit rating, our choice of career, our hair color, how clean our home is, whether or not we hit the gym faithfully—you get the idea. When it comes to another human being, we can't control whether or not he'll be attracted to us or recognize our scintillating wit, effusive personality, or all-around fabulosity. No matter how hard we wish or how good a person we may be, deadlines don't apply to the emotional side of life. Those of us unwilling to accept this can become hell-bent on the pieces of our life coming together like a puzzle, and if that means forcing a piece that doesn't *quite* fit into place, well then, so be it.

Pamela Paul, author of *The Starter Marriage and the Future of*

Matrimony and an editor at *American Demographics,* says her research shows that "the most common time for a marriage to end in divorce is in the first five years. And of those early divorces, about one-quarter end within two years."

Why are all these people getting divorced a nanosecond after they are married? The answer (for many) is pretty simple: They fell victim to their unrealistic expectations. They made a decision based on their script, rather than carefully considering if they had a relationship and a partner that could go the distance.

From Val

Of all the headaches and heartaches that are part of the Bridal Wave, the timeline was by far the one that hit me the hardest. My anxiety about being single forever paled in comparison to the timetable stranglehold I put on myself and, later, my relationship.

I always wanted to be a "young" mom, which at seventeen meant married by twenty-four with a baby at twenty-seven. At twenty-two, I adjusted that to married by twenty-seven, baby by thirty—twenty-seven being my Goldilocks number, not too young and not too old. I kept the master plan to myself, as I believe most women do, but as it shifted to keep pace with the fact that I was still single, I felt like I had somehow failed myself. Eventually, it became easier to tell myself I wasn't ever getting married, so the timeline no longer applied.

Little did Tommy know when we started dating around my twenty-fifth birthday that he had reawak-

ened the deadline-oriented beast inside me. Things were good: I loved him. He loved me. We talked about our future using the royal "we." Marriage and even children were common topics of conversation. The only thing we didn't talk about? Timing. Sure, we would be married in the future, but when did the future meet the present? Suddenly, the timeline that had faded into the distance was back with a vengeance: married by twenty-seven, baby by thirty might actually be doable. The math was easy: I needed just under a year to plan a wedding, at least a year of wedded bliss, and nine months of pregnant time. I quickly realized that I was not dealing with a lot of spare time. The problem? I knew that Tommy had to propose within the year for me to make my timeline, but Tommy had no idea that he was on such a tight schedule.

Why didn't I take control of the situation? I'm a strong, educated, career-oriented woman. In my mind, every time I talked about wanting to get married, however obliquely, I feared I would make the proposal count less. Crazy, right? I wanted Tommy to adhere to my baby-by-thirty scheme, but I wanted him to do it on his terms—as long as "his terms" meant "very soon." I was mad at him for not proposing and mad at myself for being mad at him for not proposing.

Plenty of tense moments followed in the coming months. I was nuts. With my superobvious hints about what a great location Hawaii would be for a wedding ("Did you know that in Hawaii you can get married the same day you decide to? Why, we could just decide to do it today. Wouldn't that be spontaneous?"), I was as subtle as a bull in a china shop. Tommy did eventually pop the question. But was it worth all of the anxiety? Not for me. I'm lucky that Tommy stuck it out with me.

Are You Sticking to a Script? Telltale Signs You're a Slave to a Timeline

1. When your new beau stops to pet a dog on the street, you say dreamily, "I bet you'll make a great dad."
2. The first page of the paper you turn to is the wedding announcements, where you check out everyone's age and lament how unfair life is.
3. "I always thought I'd be married by now" has gone through your head more times than you can count.
4. You think thirty-five is "over the hill" and if you aren't married by then, you might as well just give up.
5. You've considered joining JDate, the online dating site for Jewish singles, even though you're Catholic.
6. You have a hard time concentrating on first dates because you are busy computing a work-back schedule in your head: if this guy is *the one,* you can still have a baby by thirty-two . . . so long as he doesn't mind a brief courtship.
7. You are ready to issue an ultimatum.
8. You have a wedding binder full of ideas so that when he does pop the question you won't have to waste time figuring out what you like. You can hit the ground running.

9. You've always dreamed of getting married at a church that happens to have a yearlong waiting list, so you reserve your dream date for two years from now, just in case.

10. On first dates you suggest playing Twenty Questions: "Would you bring up children according to any religion?" "When do you see yourself getting married?"

Timeline Triggers

Certain life events have a way of evoking the timeline panic in even the most laid back ladies. These are pretty hard to avoid—like say, everyone you know is getting married (why else would you be reading this book?)—but sometimes calling them what they are can help you deal. These triggers are not one size fits all. Maybe you're the girl who lives for her thirtieth birthday so you can finally leave the awkward prolonged-adolescence stage behind for full-blown womanhood, or maybe when you bought a condo the furthest thing from your mind was "I always thought I'd be doing this with a husband." But in all likelihood, there are some life stages headed your way that may set you off into a rambling mess of failed expectations about "I was supposed to . . ." and "I never thought I'd be . . .":

1. **"I'd always thought I'd be married, or at least engaged, when I turned thirty."** Okay, it is a big birthday. We act like being in our twenties is a world of difference from being in our thirties, even if being in our twenties was all of two years ago. For one thing, people start tossing around the F-word—*fertility*. As in, ticktock. But thirty

also seems to be that milestone that makes us reflect on where we thought we'd be when we were "grown-ups." We equate thirty with adulthood, and most of our ideas about being adults are bound up with being married. But these days, thirty is not over the hill. In fact, if you've spent the last few years of your twenties getting your crap together, it's going to be a time of incredible independence for you. Hopefully, your career is on track, you've got some assets accumulating, and you've become an adult on your own terms, not just because you wear a wedding band. We promise you won't turn into a pumpkin on your thirtieth. Carpe diem, baby.

2. **"I always thought I'd be married by the time I was ready to buy a place."** Of course you aren't going to sit around and wait for a ring before building equity, but chances are that when you thought about owning your first home, you didn't exactly picture going to the closing and scouring Home Depot for just the right towel rack by yourself. It's a big step, and sure, it would be nice if there were someone to share the responsibility with, but buying a home is not an act of resignation because *clearly* you're never going to get married or a symbol that you're doomed to be single. It's a smart investment that you can paint whatever color you want and possibly double your money when you sell five years later.

3. **"I always thought my mother or father would get to see me walk down the aisle."** The death of a parent is probably the most shell-shocking "I'm really a grown-up" moment. Confronting mortality head-on is like inviting Father Time in to reexamine your past, present, and fu-

ture. Just remember, you've come a long way, and you still have a long way to go. An unexpected death should only prove that there's no time to waste on people and things you don't really love or can't really control.

4. **"I always thought I'd have kids at the same time as my best friend."** You haven't even surfaced from the Bridal Wave, and now your siblings and your friends are already popping them out! When the Baby Wave strikes, the fear surfaces that you'll always be "Aunt _____," the one with lint-encrusted gum stuck to the bottom of her purse who never got married. But before you go into timeline over-drive and reconnect with an ex, remember that, like getting married, having a baby is not a race. Let your friends figure out motherhood first so that when it is your time they'll be able to help. Like marriage, you definitely want to be ready for this one, because there's no going back.

The Dangers of Sticking to a Script

Notice that we have mentioned quite a few times that timeline triggers can lead to making bad decisions. Fixating on where you thought you'd be by a certain point in your life means you aren't focusing on the right things. Nowhere is this more evident than in relationships. We're talking about the girls who get so caught up in their timeline expectations that they either stay in a bad relationship or start reflecting on the "ones who got away" (generally accompanied by a curious amnesia of how or why they kicked someone to the curb in the first place). Look, we're all for perseverance where there's going to be a payoff—but not when you're committed to staying in a relationship that even a blind man could see didn't have a bright future, rather than accepting the fact that it's time to start over from scratch.

Ending it with Mr. Wrong is scary, especially when all of your friends are hooked up with guys of their own. How many fantastic women do you know who are dating guys who aren't worthy of them? Or are hanging on to guys with as much personality as a head of cauliflower? What is going on?

Number One Symptom of the Timeline: We Settle

When the Bridal Wave hits, many of us start lowering our standards—and we don't mean letting go of the six-feet, two-inch, hazel-eyed, sandy-haired, rowed-crew-in-college checklist for potential mates, we mean the basic criteria we have for relationships. The pressure forces us to accept a less-than-satisfying situation or convinces us that it's normal to "stick things out" when we're past twenty-five. Think we're exaggerating? Check out the guys below and see if any sound familiar to you.

Mr. Comfortable

Twenty-six-year-old Anna has been dating Jamie since their sophomore year of college. He's a great guy, and everyone knows it. Their families' engagement hints are becoming less and less subtle, but Anna herself isn't so sure. "I think sometimes it's better to meet someone when you're twenty-five or twenty-six, and then fall in love and get married. You need to go through college and all the crappy relationships and the cheating on each other and the starter jobs first. I've been with Jamie for five years, and at this point, couples that met years after we did are getting married. I know he loves me and I love him and there's a definite comfort factor, but I can't imagine agreeing to spend the rest of my life with him. It's not about finding someone 'better.' I don't think I'm going to find anyone 'better.' But we grew up together—and I just wonder if we'd ever find other people that we'd be happier with. At a recent wedding where I was a bridesmaid, some of my friends took me aside to let me know they were 'concerned' about me. 'He's going to find someone else if you don't marry him soon,' they said. I'm too scared to break up with him because what if I don't find someone else who's as good of a guy? But I'm also too scared to commit."

Jamie is Anna's Mr. Comfortable. Like a well-worn pair of jeans that you can't bring yourself to throw out, there's history there. And love. That's what makes it really tough. The thinking with Mr. Comfortable is that there's nothing wrong, per se. But the problem is that "nothing's wrong" isn't synonymous with "everything's right." Anna recognizes that postcollege is a key period in personal development and that she and Jamie have stopped growing together. Anna loves Jamie and knows that "on paper," he's perfect. But she already has a sneaking suspicion that their happiest future as individuals may not be together. If the pressure from family and friends and Anna's own fears about ending up alone push her to accept Jamie's proposal, she will always wonder what else might be out there, which isn't really fair to Jamie or to herself.

Are you with Mr. Comfortable?

1. When you describe him to friends, you could just as easily be describing the family dog (loyal, dependable).
2. You'd rather have a lukewarm relationship than be alone. Sex isn't *that* important.
3. You haven't made an active decision to spend your life with him, but the years just keep going by.
4. You've experienced that moment when a switch is flipped and you realize he's not "it" for you, but you're too scared to break up and see him move on.

Mr. Understudy

If you're worried about missing a deadline, you may find yourself reconsidering the guy who liked you whom you had no interest in but you know you could have at your doorstep with one phone call. Sure, you aren't totally attracted to him, but he always sends you a Christmas card, remembers your birthday, and takes you out to nicer restaurants than your past three boyfriends did. When Grandma dies, he attends the funeral with you, because after all, he loved Gram too. Your relatives are fond of saying "What a nice young man" while simultaneously giving you "What the hell is wrong with you?" looks. As another year goes by and you're both still single, you start thinking that maybe they're right. Maybe you should just settle for him. At least that way you won't be alone forever, right? And you always wanted to have kids, and so does he.

Mr. Understudy can be quite tempting when you're feeling particularly lonely or bummed about your single status. He's been waiting in the wings for his cue, and he's prepped to play the part. Marrying Mr. Understudy may get you to the church on time, but no matter how perfect your life will look to everyone else, you're the one who has to live your life day in and day out. Do you really want to live a life of settling for just okay? Mr. Understudy is a great guy, and you'll never be able to love him the way he deserves to be loved. He'll eventually realize this and (a) may cheat on you when he meets someone who *does* think he's the bees' knees or (b) divorce you when his self-esteem can't take it anymore.

Mr. Just-Needs-a-Push

Some of us strain to see "talent" or "a diamond in the rough" when we're casting the role of hubby. Your guy has some issues, but he talks the big talk and you believe in him. But staying in a relationship too long because you're seeing what he *could be* instead of what he actually *is* is a major mistake—unless you happen to have a working crystal ball, in which case who cares about this bozo? Gaze into that thing and play the stock market!

Carla met Jim at the end of junior year in college. His artfully tousled hair and ironic tee reminded her of the lead singer of her favorite band. "He was a philosophy major—the first night I met him we stayed up till dawn talking about everything. He was so different from the guys in my premed program. His plan was to go to law school, and he said we'd get married after that. He moved with me to San Francisco, where I started med school, and claimed he was going to take the year off and study for his LSATs. So he registered at a temp agency and started working for a recruiting company. Now it's five years later, and I'm done with school—and he hasn't even taken the LSATs! I bought him the Princeton Review book and offered to help him study, but it just sat there, collecting dust. I think he's a little lost." You think? "But he's *sooo* smart," she'll tell you. Great. But what is he really doing with that? Carla's life has changed dramatically in the past five years, while Jim's has flatlined. Their relationship is in limbo because he's camped out there.

"Someday" is great, but if he isn't taking steps today to get there, he's not walkin' the walk.

Is your man Mr. Just-Needs-a-Push?
1. Someday he's going to start to write that novel, but he seems to know an awful lot about *Judge Judy* for someone who claims to be dedicated to his "craft."
2. You find yourself constantly defending him to all of your friends (and not just the bitchy ones).
3. He's got a lot of opinions about how everyone else is a "sellout" but has no problem letting them pick up the tab.

Some women like playing captain, but if he refuses to step up to the plate, call a time-out and reconsider your relationship.

Number Two Symptom of the Timeline: We Go Back to the Well

Stress over a looming birthday or lonely holiday season could send you looking into your reserves to see whom you may have missed or judged too quickly, or who may have "changed." Recycling is an excellent global initiative, but it's definitely not a successful relationship strategy. You may be able to revive those cowboy boots from high school when Western is hot again, but you can't retrieve a relationship from the cast-off bin just because the clock is ticking. Leave them where they belong, in your past.

Mr. Transformer*

"Bobby is a totally different guy now. He's really getting his life together." You ran into him at the supermarket, and he looked . . . good. Apparently he gets up *before* noon now, and instead of watching videos all day on the couch, he watches videos all day in the video store, where he's held a job down for more than six months. Sure, he still lives at home and lets his mom do his laundry and make his lunch. One call to Bobby and he could be "yours" again, and just in time to make your timeline, but do you *really* want to be the one making him PB&J for lunch? Leave him with his mommy.

Mr. Boomerang

You dated and broke up for a valid reason (nine times out of ten you did the dumping). Like a habit you can't seem to break, you keep getting back together with him, however briefly, because:

1. Every time you see him you remember all the good times.
2. He keeps coming around. He's at the parties you go to, the

*Also known as "Mr. Just-Needs-a-Push" when you date him the first time.

museum opening you snuck into. If you have so much in common, maybe he is really the one. It's like fate, right?

3. The sex is good.
4. He knows you inside and out—you don't have to explain why you love Indian food but can't stand Thai.

Mr. Boomerang comes sailing back to you and makes you think, "Hey, this is great!"—great except for the fact that he cuts you off in conversation, has a wandering eye, and thinks you have issues with your parents, when he is the one who refuses to refer to his mother by anything other than "the woman who gave birth to me." The problem with a boomerang is that you broke up with him for a reason! It's just like that itchy wool sweater you pull out of the back of your closet thinking, *I forgot I had this!* It's supercute and the color rocks, but thirty minutes after leaving the house you are breaking out in hives and figuring out how to "discreetly" scratch your boobs in public.

If time is your concern, getting back together with your boomerang could not be a worse decision. You know how it's going to end: he'll do that thing that drove you crazy when you were dating and you will break up with him. Again. Now, *that* is a waste of time.

A New Species of Wrong to Look Out For: Mr. Wife-Shopper

Jill was fixed up by her sister-in-law with a lawyer who was eight years older—"a real catch—he's just been made partner!"

Listen Up, Ladies!

Men don't change their stripes. If you were unhappy with him before, you'll be unhappy with him ten years from now. Making him get rid of his peg-leg pants is fine, but you shouldn't embark on a relationship with someone as a makeover project. Redo your bathroom, not the dud you think would be "perfect" with a new job/personality/set of values.

He took her to a fancy restaurant, and things seemed to be going swimmingly until Jill noticed that something was a little off. Throughout dinner, he would drop questions like "Do you sail? My firm sponsors the regatta every year." After she told him about breaking her leg while learning to ski, he replied, "I see. What about cancer? Any cancer or mental illness in the family?" When she mentioned her desire for a puggle puppy, he asked, "How many kids do you see in your future?" and "How do you feel about stay-at-home moms?" It became evident to Jill that this guy was looking for a twenty-seven-year-old wife to go along with his golf clubs and summer home.

Is your guy on a wife hunt?

1. He's fishing around for your genetic profile before you've even had a first kiss.

2. Your first conversation covered hereditary diseases, religion, and child-rearing philosophies but not your career, hobbies, or friends.

3. He mentions that he bought an engagement ring when he turned thirty and he's been looking for a finger to put it on ever since.

After the Breakup

Now that you've learned about settling and recycling, there are a few more things we want to talk about when it comes to how you view yourself—and your relationships—during the Bridal Wave years. Yes, breakups suck in a major way. And being alone when you're navigating a busy wedding season feels like a cruel twist of fate. The first thing we need to clear up: if a substantial relationship you thought was going to end in "I do" instead ends in "It's over," *You. Have. Not. Missed. Your. Last. Chance.*

Ms. Resignation: I Guess It's Never Going to Happen for Me

Grace, thirty-two, had been dating George for six years. They had had a volatile relationship, but when he presented her with a diamond and they started planning a wedding, she assumed it'd be smoother sailing. (Why? You might ask. We have no idea!) Grace had spent the last half of her twenties with George and had always imagined she'd be married and en route to having her first child by thirty-five. But three months before the wedding, they broke it off. Now, Grace handled what was a devastating breakup with amazing fortitude (she only sat at home in her fat pants crying into pint after pint of Häagen-Dazs for about a week), but we were distressed at her sense of resignation: "I'm almost thirty-three, and with a broken engagement, I guess I have to just accept that it didn't happen for me."

Here is a smart, beautiful woman (Grace also competes in triathlons) who is already condemning herself to a life of loneliness simply because the guy she thought was "the one" didn't end up as her husband. Hear us out, Grace: we know you got hooked on drama during your breakup-to-makeup relationship, but really, all is not lost at thirty-three. If you were counseling a friend of yours, would you *really* put your hand on her shoulder and say, "Sorry, I guess it just didn't happen for you"? Hurricane George, as your friends called him, sucked up all the energy you had because a lot was wrong with your relationship from almost the beginning (hence the four breakups—two in public—leading up to the final showdown!). Sure, he was a good sparring partner, but you weren't preparing for a fencing match. If you had gone through with the wedding, it wouldn't necessarily have been the ticket to the married-and-pregnant-by-thirty-five happiness you had fantasized about.

Ms. Resentment: I Can't Believe I Wasted All Those Years!

Kristi broke up with her boyfriend, Brett, after ten years, when she realized he just wasn't going to marry her. She couldn't get over the fact that she had spent her entire twenties with him: "They were *wasted* on him! Now I'm thirty-one, but it's like I'm right back where I started at nineteen, except now all of the guys my age are either married or in relationships." Kristi was so focused on what she lost that she blocked out all of the good things that came out of the relationship.

During those ten years, Kristi learned a lot about what her priorities are, what *her* hang-ups are, and what she ultimately needs in a partner. She was so scared of being on her own after having a boyfriend for so long that she prolonged ending the relationship. Postbreakup, Kristi discovered that she loved living alone. She realized that Ikea dressers aren't that hard to assemble and that she can hang a shelf (and have it be level) as well as any man.

How to know if you really are wasting your time
1. Whenever he introduces you to a female co-worker, the word "girlfriend" drops from his vocabulary.
2. Eight months into the relationship you meet his friends— and they have no idea he has a girlfriend.
3. When you get teary-eyed at your best friend's wedding, he turns to you and says, "So is it open bar?"

Just because a relationship ends does not mean that it was a mistake or a waste of time. The only real waste of time is the time we spend on men whom we know deep down are Mr. Wrong.

4. When you plan a romantic ski weekend in Vermont, he invites his friends to "crash out on the couch. That's cool, right?"
5. He's holding on to his pizza delivery job because he doesn't want any "nine-to-five thing" getting in the way of his band's gigs—like his nephew's bar mitzvah.
6. When his parents come to town, he doesn't want you to meet them. Besides, his ex is joining them for dinner, because, "you know, they stayed in touch."
7. You get a promotion and call him to share your good news. His response: "Guess dinner's on you tonight!"
8. Whenever he talks about a married buddy, he makes a whipping gesture with his hand and the accompanying sound effect.

9. You're a year into the relationship, and you're still calling him to make plans if you want to see him on a weekend.
10. He doesn't tell you he loves you on at least a semiregular basis.

Learning to Improvise: Life Can't Be Read off a TelePrompTer

No part of our lives goes according to plan, and thank God for that. Imagine how boring life would be otherwise. (Have you ever noticed that women who *do* stick to the script seem pretty damn miserable?) The time you missed your train when you were backpacking in England and ended up sleeping in a field with three of your best friends? Best night of the trip. If your plan went something like "get married, buy a house, have babies," we aren't suggesting that you lose your aspirations, but be prepared to flip the order. These are separate goals and not necessarily chronological ones.

You can't control when you are going to meet the man of your dreams, so why waste so much energy stressing out on it? The magical part of being young (and yes, even in your thirties, you are still young!) is that anything can happen at any time. Of course, when you walk in on your boyfriend making out with your best friend, you may not be thinking, "Wow, how magical!" Allowing yourself to be open to new experiences will help you break free of your script. Besides, guys can smell women on a manhunt a mile away. (We're convinced it's one of those things they teach them when they separate you for sex ed in sixth grade.) Fixating on amorphous things like "finding Mr. Right" is time better spent on figuring out who you are as a person and learning how to be happy on your own, so that when you do stumble into a Mr. Right you will be together for the right reasons. Knowing that you are fine on your own will give you the strength to end what isn't working and the time to nurture what is. Instead of obsessing about the future, live for today.

Man or no man, the thirty things you should do before you're out of your thirties.
1. Travel to a different continent.
2. Learn to speak a new language.
3. Complete a marathon (walk, run, or crawl, but cross the finish line).
4. Own a pet.
5. Invest in eye cream.
6. Skydive.
7. Live alone.
8. Perfect one dish. No one has to know it's the only thing you can cook.
9. Get at least one degree.
10. Reconcile all your differences with your parents (the teens breed them).
11. Travel within your country. Take the time to get to know where you're from.
12. Ask for a raise.
13. Start an IRA or 401(k) and contribute the max—lots of compound interest.
14. Go to Italy to change your perspective.
15. Move out of your parents' house.

16. Revel in your great body because you'll never have it again.

17. Drop friends who are pains in the ass because in ten years they will still be pains in the ass and you'll feel too guilty to get rid of them.

18. Go to Vegas and be able to say "What happens in Vegas stays in Vegas."

19. Shop at Forever 21.

20. Quit smoking.

21. Eat dinner alone at a restaurant with no props—no books, mags, or phone calls.

22. Volunteer voluntarily (not because it's a class requirement).

23. Participate in an Indian sweat lodge.

24. Raft the Grand Canyon.

25. Pick up a new sport (in ten years your body won't let you do that).

26. Find a new way to express yourself creatively.

27. If you're professionally unsatisfied, change careers.

28. Try to contact a long-lost friend.

29. Face a phobia (or at least try to).

30. Reread your favorite childhood book.

Repeat After Us

I promise to stop dating guys who are not worthy of my time because I was "supposed" to be married by twenty-seven according to the timeline in my head. In fact, I will stop beginning sentences with the words "I was supposed to . . ." and "I never thought . . ." I do now recognize that "sticking it out" with

Mr. Wrong does nothing but let a guy get away with crappy behavior, and I'm better than that. I will recycle my newspapers and bottles, not my men. I will not think of past relationships as time wasted but rather as lessons learned. I understand that settling is fine for houses, dust, and personal injury cases but not for my love life. I will not issue an ultimatum and be the girl who says, "or else." When I am feeling time-crunched, I will not cast my bucket back into the well to see if I can dredge up something but will keep looking for the man and the relationship I know is right for me. I do know that if I'm dead set on checking off "get married" on my to-do list when I'm twenty-five, I'm statistically increasing my chances of putting "get divorced" on my list three years later. I will do my best to make peace with the fact that life is random and cannot be organized along a timeline the way I plotted the events leading up to World War I in fourth-grade social studies class.

CHAPTER 5

· · · · · · · ·

The League of Concerned Citizens

· ·

Everyone from your gyno to your mom has
an opinion about your nonmarried self.
Here's how to shut them up

· ·

Ah, Family

Who else can you count on for unconditional love and back-handed compliments? As if it weren't bad enough that your friends are dropping like flies and you're spending every other weekend at a wedding-related function, now your family feels like your romantic status (or lack thereof) is free rein. They broach the topic at Thanksgiving dinner, in the supermarket with your neighbor, when they call you on Valentine's Day to make sure you aren't too down about being alone (thanks for pointing that out!), and family weddings, when the topic of your nonimpending nuptials is on the tip of everyone's tongues. "Family weddings put me on high alert," says thirty-two-year-old Keiko, who has been dating her boyfriend for going on four years now. "It's like there is a conspiracy to put us on the spot. They have no idea what's really going on in our relationship but feel no qualms about turning to us and saying, 'So what about you two, when are you going to get married?' Why do they think it's their business to ask us that?"

Why are our families so obsessed with the fourth finger on our left hand? Do they enjoy trying to make us feel like an ant under a magnifying glass? Let's hope not. What feels to you like an interrogation is their genuine interest in your life and concern for your well-being. And let's face it: the more years you've got under your belt, the less inhibited you tend to be about speaking your mind. But while their brutal honesty can be rude, insensitive, and alarmist, they surely don't see it as the intensely personal prodding it actually is—or realize that their "helpful" hints are coming at you during a time when you are getting the same message from everyone. So we're here to tell you that for once in your life "It's not *you*, it's *them*" is absolutely true.

The Grand Inquisition: What They're <u>Really</u> Thinking, and How to Politely Give Them a Piece of <u>Your</u> Mind, Too

What they say: When are you two going to get married?

What they mean: What's wrong with you, him, or your relationship that you can't make it legal?

What you say: Everything's going great with our relationship. We are committed to each other and have a great life together, so we don't really feel a pressing need. If we change our minds, we'll let you know.

What you mean: Mind your own business. After all, what do you know about marriage? Your husband has been sleeping on the couch since the Carter administration!

What they say: Seeing anyone special yet?
What they mean: Is there something wrong with you? Are you gay?
What you say: Let's not talk about me. Great Aunt Jean was telling me you have hemorrhoids. How's that going?
What you mean: Back off, lady. You don't want to mess with this bull.

What they say: You remember Bill, that nice boy from your high school? He's a podiatrist now. Very successful, too.
What they mean: You should have said yes when he asked you to the prom. Now you're going to be an old maid.
What you say: Really, how great for him. Did you run into him when you were getting your bunion surgery?
What you mean: Don't start what you don't want to finish, because I *will* go there.

What they say: How's that Tom guy you used to go with? Or Bart? They seemed like nice guys.
What they mean: Are you too picky? Can't you keep a relationship?
What you say: They were great guys, except for Tom's gambling habit and Bart's felony charges. I thought I could do better than that. Don't you?
What you mean: You have no idea about my life.

What they say: My neighbor Gladys's son Gary is such a nice fellow. Why don't I give him your number?

What they mean: He's a dateless loser like you. You'd be perfect together!

What you say: Thanks for thinking of me, but I'm actually seeing a few different people right now.

What you mean: I'd rather stay in and watch reruns of *Full House* than spend an evening with someone you think is a catch.

What they say: Don't you want kids someday?

What they mean: Are you one of those child-hating women I've heard about? If not, your ovaries are drying up as we speak.

What you say: Of course. But I feel that since I have been so blessed, I should adopt a child who is already on this earth and just needs a good home to thrive in.

What you mean: Zip it, lady. Just because you're stuck changing diapers and making goo-goo talk at your two-year-old doesn't mean I have to give up my freedom to join your club.

HINT

Be Careful—Choose Your Moment to Get Nasty

Otherwise, you'll come off more as angry, bitter girl than fun, sassy girl. Just because your family is rude and insensitive to your feelings doesn't mean that you always have to stoop to their level of passive-aggressive communication.

Caution! Bridal Wave Danger Zones

Some may argue that any encounter with someone who shares your DNA is a BWDZ, but certain run-ins are more hazardous than others and require adequate preparation. Never go into the battlefield unarmed.

BWDZ 1: The holidays. The most wonderful time of the year?

Religious celebrations are prime time for your family to hit you with some Bridal Wave whoppers.

How to get through the visit without any scenes at the dinner table, around the Christmas tree or Hanukkah bush, or in the return line at Best Buy

1. **Preempt.** This requires some planning, but consider sending an end-of-year letter. Put it out there for everyone to see on your own terms. "I am still with the guy that my family thinks is wasting my time, and yes, we are happy, and no, I am not worried that he will never pop the question." A strong offense will cause the recipients to play defense, by either shutting them up or forcing them to say things like "We never said that! Whatever gave you that idea?"

2. **Hide.** If you live far from home and the holidays have become more unpleasant than pleasant in recent years, consider taking a year off. Thanksgiving is one holiday that you can easily do with friends without offending your family. After all, the four-day weekend is the worst time of

the year to travel, and since it's so close to Christmas and Hanukkah, you'll be seeing them soon enough anyway. Or find a like-minded single pal and plan a Caribbean get-away during the Christmas break. You'll get a real vacation *and* a tan. Your family may give you the guilt trip, but rest assured, your married brother who's been housebound with his flu-stricken kids will be seething with jealousy and wish he could have done the same thing.

3. **Anticipate.** Think ahead to what bullets might be fired your way and prepare some answers. That way when your grandmother looks at your bitten-to-the-quick nails and says, "No wonder you're single, with hands like those," it will seem like cake compared to the worse-comes-to-worst scenario you imagined.

4. **Accentuate the positive.** Go in determined to stay up-beat. How many awkward comments can you grin through? How many conversations can you deflect? For example, "Why is it you never have a boyfriend to bring home for Thanksgiving?" could be redirected cheerfully with "I see you all so rarely that I want to spend this time really catching up with you on your lives. How is that bankruptcy coming anyway, Aunt Helen?"

5. **Are you ready for some football?** Generally the women drop the insensitive bombs. Sitting around watching sports with the guys is much safer territory.*

---

*To do this successfully, you will need to know what you are talking about so you can seem genuinely interested and avoid being tossed out. Nobody wants to watch a football game with a girl who keeps on asking questions or who comments on how lame it is that those guys are dressed up like Bengals and Pirates.

If you are feeling like one is the loneliest number and the yuletide is anything but bright, check out these ways to get your jolly on.

1. **One for them, one for me.** When holiday shopping, don't forget yourself. 'Tis the season for giving, of course, but who says you can't give to the most important person in your life, you?

2. **Do-gooder.** Volunteering during the holidays is a good way to check your head. It helps you to focus on everything you do have, not everything you don't.

3. **Smokin' (hot, that is).** If you'd rather snort eggnog up your nose than hit another holiday party alone, try buying a fun new dress and be the hottest girl in the room. Let everyone else wear Santa Claus–and reindeer-themed sweaters. You can be the sexy single one who makes them feel frumpy.

4. **Deck your halls.** Put on some sappy seasonal music, and make your place holiday-ready with twinkling lights, a wreath on the door, seasonal potpourri (that doesn't smell like anything you've ever encountered in nature), and glittery candles. Better yet, invite a friend over to help you decorate—preferably one with a knack for interior design or wreath making.

5. **Better them than me.** When your siblings start to marry and procreate, the holiday vibe shifts to being all about your nieces and nephews. Instead of going to your parents' house, you may be invited to your sister's or brother's, where you will get to see firsthand exactly what you are missing. A dose of diaper changing, tantrum throwing, and the never-ending loop of children's Christmas music is usually good medicine for our nonmarried

selves. Nothing better than being able to give a screeching baby back to its parents and going home to your own clean, nonchildproofed home.

Believe It or Knot

Lip service

Think of this the next time you're the only one with nobody to smooch with under the mistletoe: "mis-tel" is the Anglo-Saxon word for "dung." Essentially, our modern word "mistletoe" means "dung-on-a-twig,"[1] because people once believed that the parasitic plant would bud spontaneously on twigs where birds left a little something. Here's to kissing under the crap! (Thanks, About.com.)

Gaggle of female relatives + mimosas = BWDZ 2

"When my younger cousin got engaged, my aunt threw her a tea party–themed bridal shower. Most of the guests were relatives who I hadn't seen in a while," says Natalie, twenty-eight. "When I headed out to the patio, I found myself face-to-face with an audience of older women in giant hats. I didn't even know most of their names, but there they were, frantically asking 'What about you?' 'Time is running out. You need to have a baby by thirty.' 'Are you dating?' 'Are you really looking?' Talk about the Mad Hatter firing squad! I instantly went into comedian mode. I made a joke that my roommate, Suzy, was like my boyfriend/husband: 'I go out with her. On Fridays we're both tired after a long week, so we have Friday night movie dates.' That really freaked them out. 'Don't joke like that! You have to separate, or else you'll never meet someone. You have to start getting serious!' " Humor is an admirable defense tactic, but it didn't provide the conversation ender Natalie was hoping for.

Stop-them-in-their-tracks-move: Natalie's options

1. **Miss Manners.** First, she could have said, "Thanks for your concern, but today is really about Beth. Let's focus on her instead." From there she could turn toward Beth and ask her a question about her honeymoon. This would give her at least a three-minute break as the bride went into detail about her week in [fill in sunny tropical island name here], sending the Mad Hatters off her trail.

2. **Fire with Fire.** Natalie could have shot back with "That may have been true in your day, but I would rather wait to get married until I have found the right man, not just a man who meets an arbitrary deadline. You know what I mean, right, Aunt Edna? After all, your first marriage ended terribly and then you were left penniless to raise Joann on your own while he got away with hiding all of the money in an offshore account. What a shame." Then she could smile sweetly and delicately sip her tea.

3. **The Educator.** Natalie could have also paused and smiled around at all of them before saying "I feel so grateful to have been born when I was. Women my age have so many more options than you did. I'm able to do what I want when I want, and I have another decade to worry about children. It's really a great time to be a woman."

4. **The Steamroller.** Or Natalie could have taken a tip from our friend Tad and ignored the chatter. Tad's family's favorite question is when he will propose to his long-term girlfriend. Tad's highly developed technique? "I just railroad over the conversation. I refuse to engage in the discussion at all." He swears that it works like a charm.

BWDZ 3: Your younger sis is getting to the altar first, and your family won't let you forget it

A younger sister or brother getting married can set the League into action on your behalf whether you're in a relationship or not. Maya, thirty-three and in a long-term relationship, can't understand why her relatives don't get that their questions cause more harm than good. "Watching my younger sister get married and having to field offhanded remarks from my mom like 'Who would have thought your *younger* sister would get married first?' and 'Do you think that going to all these weddings is giving him any ideas?' or my favorite from my younger, now married and 'all-knowing,' sis, 'Maybe you shouldn't have moved in with him so quickly,' which only led to tension in my otherwise perfectly happy relationship with Ryan."

Stop-them-in-their-tracks move: Stay above the fray. Try something like "It's about time she did something first. She copied me our entire lives, learning from my mistakes and successes. Now it's time for her to take the lead for a bit." Keep it light and happy. You don't want your younger sis to catch wind of the awkwardness or have her feel like she is somehow breaking the chain of command by getting married before you.

BWDZ 4: *Your younger sis is getting to the altar first, and* you *can't forget it*

Remember *The Brady Bunch*? After the show ended, there was a special called "The Brady Brides." The plot went like this: Middle sis Jan was engaged to be married, which sent the oldest one, Marcia, over the edge. She was so upset that her younger sibling was getting married first that she met and got engaged to a man in time to change Jan's big day to a double wedding.

Some women couldn't care less if their younger sibs get hitched first, but others head straight to Marcia territory when they hear the news. After all, not only did you do everything first (puberty, driver's license, prom), but you also blazed the way with your parents. Technically, you made things easier for them. How dare they go and steal your thunder by asking you to be maid of honor, right?

How to deal: Well, you may still see your sis as the ingrate who enjoyed a midnight curfew when she was sixteen due only to your lobbying efforts and savvy negotiating skills, but the reality is that you are both (more or less—we know all about the prolonged-adolescence thing) adults. Remember our little talk about being last? Marriage. Is. Not. A. Race.

BWDZ 5: *"I'm only staying alive so I can see you walk down the aisle": When Grandma attacks*

Twenty-six-year-old Riley told us that her grandmother has been pestering her about getting hitched. "She keeps saying she won't be around for that much longer, so I better hurry up. She also said, 'You're not going be young forever. He might be your last chance at getting married.' " Listen, Grams, we appreciate the concern but Riley's going to be just fine. In 1947, being unmarried at twenty-six after going with a guy might have been the kiss of death. But that was a different world. To be an independent, happy, successful woman able to buy her own home and provide for herself was an anomaly for our grandparents. "That generation definitely still has a hard time processing that a woman can be perfectly financially stable on her own and so can a guy. Marriage for them is still about having that much more in the bank," says Samantha, twenty-nine. Educate your elders on the wonders of modern life and remind them that with the life expectancy rates these days, you've got plenty of time and are in no hurry to settle. And practice patience. Nobody wants to scream at Grandma.

Then again, sometimes they deserve it. Imagine this: sitting around the head table at her younger cousin's wedding, Jane's great-aunt (grandmother of the bride) asked her about her love life. No, Jane told her, she wasn't seeing anyone, to which Great-aunt Mary replied (brace yourself), "I guess you are just going to be an old maid career woman." Thankfully, Jane had a biting wit and replied, "Would you rather I marry an asshole who treats me like crap?" Her reply shut Great-aunt Mary up, but the words "old maid career woman" struck at the core of Jane. She would never admit it to anyone, but her aunt voiced her greatest fear. That's why family can drive us crazy—in a blink of an eye they can fire an arrow straight into our Achilles' heel.

The League of Concerned Citizens' Ruthless Leader: Mommy Dearest

You are not your mother (thank God!)

How many times has your mother reminded you where she was in her life when she was your age? As in "When I was your age I had a five-year-old and an infant!" Upon hearing this (again) you're probably filled with disbelief, not envy. You're still figuring out who you are and what you want in life—imagine doing that with two kids, a husband, and a mortgage! Fact is, most of our moms didn't have the luxury of choices that we do. Of course, our family members don't always value the choices we make. But that's why they are our decisions to make and not theirs.

Many of our moms would argue that our choices are overrated. When they look at us in our cramped apartments, they might not see an independent woman who is thrilled to bits to no longer have a roommate. They see an overpriced, depressing box that we are spending time in only when we aren't working at our sixty-hour-a-week jobs.

Try opening up your life to your mom. Invite her over for a games night with some of your friends. Order in, have a potluck, or cook dinner for your pals and let her see you in your element. And don't hide the clutter. Show her that part of the fun of being single is that no one is expecting the dishes in the sink to be done immediately after you eat.

Sometimes Mother does *know best*

Raquel and Juan grew up in the same small town in Ohio. Though they were in the same grade, their worlds hardly intersected. Raquel was the popular prom queen, while Juan was the stereotypical nerd. Flash forward ten years. Grocery shopping one day, Raquel's mom bumped into Juan's mom as they reached for the same head of cabbage. They hadn't seen each other in years, but they quickly caught up, realized that their children were both single, and decided that the kids should connect, despite the three thousand miles that separated them. They swapped their children's e-mail addresses and immediately directed their children to drop the other a line. To stop his mother's harping, Juan sent a short note to Raquel that began, "My mom told me to write to you . . ." Lo and behold, Raquel and Juan got married after a whirlwind romance. As part of their wedding, they read from those first e-mails. It's easy to discount advice and not all advice should be heeded, but sometimes you should give it a shot, because you truly never know.

The best stop-'em-in-their-tracks move: honesty

Most of the time our family members have no idea how their casual remarks and questions can feel like sucker punches. Every once in a while you have to remind them that you are doing your best and making decisions that are right for you, and you would appreciate it if they would *support* you, not add to your insecurities. "Mom, when you ask me if I think Bill is going to propose soon, it only fuels my anxiety" is clear and to the point. Remaining calm and not returning to the emotional age of the terrible twos will help you make your case. If your mom thinks you're a mess, you only reinforce that opinion by slamming doors and causing a scene. Be honest about what you are going through and what you are hoping to gain from confiding in her—her support. You know you're a grown-up when you can do this. Plus your mom just might relish the chance to be your confidante instead of just nosey old Mom.

It could be worse . . .

"My dad's always 'subtly' trying to find out if I'm gay. Last time I visited, for example, he gave me a book he'd found in the home of a now-dead relative who was single her whole life. 'She lived with a "roommate" until she died,' he said, handing it to me. 'I found this inscription. Do you think that means she was gay?' On the title page of the book—which was about gardening, by the way—it said 'Happy birthday! Love, Milly.' I'm guessing he asked me as a way to test my gaydar and my knowledge of the secret language of lesbians, in which 'Happy birthday' is code for something scandalous. Still, it's better than the time he asked if I—not my teenage brothers, mind you—had walked off with one of his *Playboys*. Ew."—Amanda, twenty-eight.

Remember This: It's Your Decision, No Matter What

Some parents are still very traditional when it comes to love and marriage, particularly if they are religious. The idea of giving it away for free and shaming the family are a little dramatic in this day and age, but some parents still have issues with co-habitation. Margaret has been living with her boyfriend, Tom, for over a decade. They have had the marriage discussion, but both 'fess up to liking being part of what Margaret calls "the Goldie Hawn Club." "We're outside the status quo. We don't need to get married to feel like we have a committed relationship." Both come from strict Catholic families who would like nothing better than to see their kids make it legal, which has put a strain on Margaret's relationship with her father. "We got a ton of pressure in the first five years we were dating. My father even refused to let us spend the night together 'under his roof' because we were living together." But she is confident in her relationship and refuses to let his anger send her to the altar. "If Tom and I do decide to get married, it will be our decision, not anyone else's."

The League's Foot Soldiers

Hearing the bridal buzz from your family is bad enough, but at least you can steel yourself for familial encounters. But what about the sneak attacks that come from such unexpected sources as your gynecologist, your boss, and, yes, even a potential landlord? Some real-life tales:

Just when you thought it was safe to get your teeth cleaned . . .

Sophie, twenty-nine, tells us, "I was at the dentist getting work done on my crown. He was busy making requisite doctor talk.

(Why do dentists try to start conversations with us anyway? Hello, your hand is in my mouth!) 'Any travel plans this summer?' he asked. 'I have so many weddings to go to, I don't even have time to take a vacation,' I said, mostly joking. He put down the plaque scraper, furrowed his brow, and said, 'Don't worry, Sophie. Your time will come.' The nerve!" Now, nobody wants to cause a scene at the dentist's office. But what's a girl to do? The easiest thing is to cut them off at the pass with a block. After all, Sophie didn't want to get into her personal life with her dentist, and who does, really? Her best bet would have been to keep it short and sweet: a smile and "Thank you. I'm sure it will, too, but right now I'm enjoying my freedom too much to settle down."

Let's be honest, Sophie left herself a little open on that one. If you don't want to field awkward questions from well-meaning semistrangers, keep things impersonal and turn questions around, something like "No concrete plans yet. And you?" Never forget that people love to talk about themselves.

. . . *Or go apartment hunting*

Jessica, thirty-one and single, decided it was time to cut her commute in half and move out of her gorgeous, unbelievably cheap one-bedroom. The first apartment she looked at had rugs that looked as antiquated as the tenants. When she saw numerous signs posted about keeping the noise level down after seven, she realized that this was basically a unit for seniors and politely hauled on out of there. She hoped the next building, in a hipper neighborhood, would be better. But after touring that apartment, she felt like it was way overpriced for what it was.

The manager, perhaps picking up on her ambivalence, told her in a conspiratorial way, "You know, a lot of doctors live in this building." Horrified, Jessica thanked the woman for her time and got out of there, whereupon she immediately sent us an e-mail detailing the event. When we spoke with her she admitted, "Well, I *would* rather live in a building with a bunch of doctors than a bunch of old folks, but do I have 'Available!' stamped on my forehead?" So there's the conundrum: Jessica *is* single and looking, but does that give everyone she encounters the right to point it out? The fact that she was apartment hunting solo shouldn't have been license for a manager to cinch the deal with the "marrying a doctor" dream.

When strangers cross the line, you have two choices:

- Ignore them and move on. You'll probably never see them again.
- Speak your mind and take one for the team.

Jessica would have to have been pretty ballsy to have shot back, "You don't even know me. What gives you the right to make such a personal suggestion? You just lost yourself a stellar tenant." The con of this tactic is that you look sort of crazy and defensive. The pro? What do you care what a stranger thinks of you? Once you turn on your heel and walk out, she'll probably think twice about using that sales strategy again—and single women everywhere will have you to thank.

After all, the League of Concerned Citizens is motivated by the assumption that if you're not married you must be unhappy about it. Prove them wrong, or shut them up for good by challenging them. It's about time people know that most women have better things to do than obsess over whether or not they are going to get married. Of course, as we discuss in the next chapter, try telling *that* to the folks in Hollywood.

Repeat After Us

I promise not to throw the centerpiece at my grandfather when he volunteers to set me up with my third cousin once removed because he says I spend too much time working to meet any eligible "suitors." I do know that my parents have my best interests at heart and if they're jonesing for grandkids, I'll remind them that they'll be trading bridge night and golf Sundays for diaper duty. I will gladly be a bridesmaid for my sister because she asks me, even though the groomsman escorting me is someone I babysat when he was five and I was twelve. When my Aunt Busybody jumps in with "And please bring Susie a man this year" right before "Amen" at Christmas dinner, I will quickly add, "And may Aunt Busybody learn that all things happen in due time," smile gracefully, and enjoy my meal. When the inappropriate questions really get to me, I will try to remember that it's not because I'm giving off a desperate single woman vibe but that my interrogators simply suffer from limited imaginations and life views. I will expand their horizons by showing that it kind of rocks that I can go to Puerto Rico with my girlfriends for Thanksgiving weekend and have a fling with the scuba instructor while they scold Junior for hurling a fistful of ambrosia salad at Aunt Vera.

CHAPTER 6

Reality Check

Does your inner voice sound suspiciously like Carrie Bradshaw? How to tune out the marriage static from pop culture

You can prepare witty retorts for the "well-meaning" relatives who make thoughtless comments about your love life. You can choose to spend more time with your not-yet-lobridemized friends, but you can't avoid the marriage static that is all around you. This becomes especially apparent just after a breakup or when you have had it up to here with your friend's constant wedding-related yammering and you yearn to breathe some bridal-free air. The magazines we pick up, the books we read, and the movies and TV shows we watch all echo the same mantra: you are not complete until you find a man and say "I do." Sure, the women's movement paved the way for us to grow up with the idea that we could do anything, but the greatest story ever told (sorry, Jesus) is still boy meets girl, boy marries girl, and together they cash in a one-way ticket to nuptial never-never land. Our parents may teach us to stand on our own two feet, but before that lesson came Snow White, Cinderella, and Sleeping Beauty—fairy tales where a handsome prince saves the day. In our teens and twenties, fairy tales make way for romantic comedies, chick lit, and reality shows where women vie for an engagement ring from a virtual stranger or stand with their hands on their dream wedding dress for days on end. We can't do anything about the fairy tales that are burned into our brain, but we can take steps to reduce our exposure to the toxic transmitters of wedding static emitting this signal: Everyone is getting married but you!

Static Source: The Church of Celebrity

When we're looking for "real-life" fairy-tale land, we don't have to go much further than the red carpet. There we'll find our witches and our princesses, our villains and our heroes. *In Touch, US, Star, OK*—the list of weekly mags that are devoted to covering celebrity culture seems to keep increasing. Even *Star,* the tabloid that we used to sneak glances of as we waited in the checkout line, has turned into a bona fide star bible, leaving behind the world of two-headed alien babies for who is hooking up with whom this week. We worship at the altar of celebrity with every dollar we spend on a crap movie because we want to see if there really was chemistry between the two lead actors who are now a couple and with every tabloid that we give in and buy. Think worship's a strong word? If you've had an actual conversation about what *really* happened to Nick and Jessica, then you know what we're talking about. Recent studies published in the *British Journal of Psychology* say that one in three people in the United States and the United Kingdom suffer from "celebrity worship syndrome." That's right, it's a psychological condition.

It's not as if we're saying that hermits are better off. Having intimate knowledge of celebrities is what ties many of us together. The crazy thing that starts to happen with all this celebrity brouhaha is that we start thinking of stars as our public peer group. Hearing about a celeb's impending nuptials can have the same results as getting our umpteenth IGBN call. Just as we compare ourselves to our friends who had the whole package (marriage, summer house, dog) by twenty-eight, we refer to celebs by first name as if they were in our extended friendship circle and chart our own progress in reference to theirs. "I used to pick up a few weeklies to 'escape,' but every time I read about another twenty-something celeb tying the knot, I would be reminded that my boyfriend of almost a decade is still uncertain about whether or not he is 'into' the idea of marriage," says Alison, who eventually forced herself to go cold turkey on the 'bloids.

Reality Check: You Are Not a Celebrity

You may envy Reese's "young mom" status and think Gwyneth eloped just the way you would have wanted to, but comparing your life to the 2-D lives that fill the pages of *Star* will get you nowhere. In fact, it's probably only going to make you unhappy. A psychologist at Leicester University found that some people would rather lose themselves in dreams of their idol than face their own lives, resulting in depression and stress.[1] We hate to break it to you, but you are not a celebrity. You don't get paid to make appearances at store openings. You don't have "people" to fetch your bottled water or pick up your dry cleaning.

Celebrities can afford to blow six digits on a wedding and then get divorced six weeks later. You can't. Besides, would you really be willing to say good-bye to carbohydrates for the rest of your life? We didn't think so. Why fixate on lifting some celeb details for your own dream day when we all know Hollywood marriages tank faster (and more often) than any civilian's? Of the celebrity weddings featured on "An *Entertainment Tonight* Event: Celebrity Weddings Unveiled," which aired in July 2005, six of the couples are already divorced—or, in the case of Sophia Bush and Chad Michael Murray,* who received an annulment after just five months of wedded bliss, *technically never married.*

Believe It or Knot

The latest Hollywood trend in marriage? No, it's not Monique Lhuillier gowns but annulments. Think Kenny and Renee, Britney and Jason Alexander, and our faves, Chad and Sophia. Different from a divorce, which legally ends a marriage, an annulment declares that a marriage never existed. How do you pretend that a marriage never happened when it's been featured in national publications? The wonders of stardom will never cease.

For fun, let's take a look at the reported costs of celebrity couplings and their ROIs (returns on investment).

---

*At the time of this writing CMM is engaged again—to a *One Tree Hill* starlet—again. We think this is one situation where guests might want to invoke the year-to-buy-a-wedding-gift clause.

Celeb Pairing	Cost of Wedding	Length of Marriage	Approximate Average Cost per Day of Wedded Bliss
Tori Spelling and what's-his-name	$1,000,000	15 months[2]	$2,173
Bennifer 1.0	$2,000,000	Canceled	Wonder what the cancellation fees on two mil are?
Brad and Jen (would that be Pittifer?)	$1,000,000	4 years	$685
Nick and Jessica	$200,000	3 years	$183
Sophia Bush and Chad Michael Murray	Vera Wang + beachfront + Santa Barbara's Bacara Resort = at least $110,000[3]	5 months	$658

ARE YOU TOO "IN TOUCH"?

Have you allocated too many brain cells to celebrity wedding details? This quiz will evaluate your risk factor. Match the marital mayhem to the celebrity.

1. Pimps and maids, enough said.
2. Given a 6.1-carat pink diamond engagement ring.

3. Was engaged to a Greek shipping heir (what does that mean, anyway?).

4. Requested that doves fly out of the trees during her ceremony.

5. Was rumored to have carried a vial of her now exhusband's blood around her neck.

6. Promised in her wedding vows to make her guy banana milk shakes.

7. Of her first wedding she said, "I have a woman's body and a child's emotions." Length of marriage? Eight months.

8. On her third marriage as of 2005. Length of shortest marriage? Eight months.

9. Divorced before their cover story in *InStyle* hit the newsstands. Length of marriage? Seven months.

10. Had her two-month marriage annulled in 2005.

11. Her stated reason for an annulment? Fraud.

12. Married a man who later had intimate relations with someone else on this list (and there's video to prove it). Length of marriage? Nine months.

Celebs: Because we have a feeling you're pretty advanced in this area, we've made it more difficult by using some answers more than once and some not at all.

A. Jennifer Lopez
B. Courtney Thorne-Smith
C. Britney Spears
D. Angelina Jolie
E. Madonna
F. Elizabeth Taylor

G. Nicky Hilton
H. Lindsay Lohan
I. Shannen Doherty
J. Nicole Ritchie
K. Paris Hilton
L. Jennifer Aniston
M. Renee Zellweger
N. Gwen Stefani

Answers: 1C, 2A, 3K, 4N, 5D, 6L, 7F, 8A, 9B, 10G, 11M, 12I

If you thought this quiz was too easy, you need to put down the *People* and get your head out of the *Star.* Quick, do you know your dad's birthday? How about your grandmother's? If you feel closer to a Hilton sister than to your own flesh and blood, you may want to take a moment to reevaluate how much of your brain is storing useless celeb trivia. Remember, the more time you spend taking in this crap, the less time you're spending actually living your life.*

Tune it out: for life beyond celebrities, get your glossy fix here.

1. **Bust: For Women with Something to Get off Their Chests.** A non-man-hating female perspective on pop culture.
2. **Swivel: The Nexus of Women and Wit.** A biannual print literary magazine devoted to smart, funny writing by smart, funny women.
3. **Entertainment Weekly.** *EW* contains surprisingly intelligent coverage of film, TV, and books minus the sycophantic celebrity angle.

*Besides, if you end up sitting next to a hot stranger, do you really want him to see you perusing the spread on "Dream Weddings of the Stars"?

4. *Self.* We love that the focus in this mag remains on you and how you can grow and achieve your personal goals, not how you can make someone else love you.

5. *Details.* Let guys debate whether or not this is a mag for metros or the truly gay; we love it because it has articles about cultural trends and relationships that puts most women's glossies to shame.

6. *Jane.* Recently remodeled, this mag is geared toward women in their twenties who are looking for more than sex secrets and celeb worship. Tips on saving cash while still living large, essays on different issues, and uncanned celebrity profiles make *Jane* worthy of a second look.

Static Source: Reality TV

And the winner gets . . . a husband!

When *Who Wants to Marry a Millionaire?* aired back in 2000, the program attracted 22.8 million viewers during its final half hour. And despite the debacle that ensued after the show (you know, that the millionaire wasn't *really* a millionaire—not to mention the cries of outrage over a beauty contest where the prize is a husband), the winner-gets-a-ring-premise continued to proliferate. *The Bachelor, The Bachelorette, Average Joe,* and *The World's Smallest Groom* all had men and women competing to be the chosen ones.

Just when it looked as though this genre had seen its day, *The Bachelor* is back—and in Paris! Though we may have been out-raged at the sacrilegious assumption that people could be married by a television audience in 2000, our ADD society is fine with it six years later, so long as they get to go on a date or two first.

What's the message behind these prime-time gems? That getting married is a competition, and you either win or lose; if it takes catty comments or getting skanky behind some bushes, so be it. But seriously, when the cameras were off, Joe Millionaire didn't look like much of a winner in our book. And considering that the bachelor franchise is one for eleven marriagewise as we go to press (the one married couple came from *The Bachelorette*), these women would have a way better shot taking their manhunt off air.

And the bridal broadcast doesn't stop with these soon-to-be-a-vague-memory reality shows. Wedding-centric documentary-style programming litters basic cable with such offerings as *A Wedding Story; Whose Wedding Is It Anyway?; Platinum Weddings; Wild Weddings; Bridezillas* . . . the list goes on and on. Sitting at home on a Saturday night (WE + Saturday night programming = evil) watching some crazy beyotch in one of these shows stomping around Atlanta screaming at her planner, it's hard not to think, *Even this chick found someone to marry her?*

You can cancel your cable subscription, but there's no avoiding the "very special" wedding episode of every sitcom, hour-long drama, and, naturally, soap opera in existence. Like a radio station you get only in certain places, you don't pick up on the signal until you are in your Bridal Wave years, when suddenly the message of these shows is loud and clear: "Everyone is getting married—except you." What's a girl to do? Thank goodness for TiVo and the following shows that break the mold.

Turn down the static: TV shows that feature women on top (not cake toppers).

1. **Buffy the Vampire Slayer.** Petite blonde with cute clothes kicked major demon ass in this legendary series.

2. **Girlfriends.** As the theme song for this show says, "My girlfriends, there through thick and thin." With friends like these, who needs a man?

3. **The Golden Girls.** Despite starring septuagenarians, this 1980s sitcom was surprisingly progressive. *SATC*'s Samantha must have learned a thing or two from Blanche. And the millions of gay men who have these DVDs in their collection can't be wrong.

4. **Alias.** Sydney Bristow is a grad student and a CIA spy, but in the first episode she discovers she's actually been working for the very people she thought she was fighting against. Warning: seasons four and five get a bit soap-opera-y, so stick to the early years.

5. **The Closer.** Newly appointed head of LAPD's Priority Murder Squad, Kyra Sedgwick's Brenda Johnson is not afraid to boss around her male subordinates or cave in to her snack-cake cravings.

Sex and the City: Friend or Foe?

Why didn't *Sex and the City* make the cut? We know, we had the Sunday-night viewing parties too. But after the last episode aired we were left wondering, is *SATC* a friend or foe to those in their Everyone-I-Know-Is-Getting-Married Years?

Friend

To a whole generation of women, *SATC* was the first real depiction of what it meant to be single in your thirties, only with way better clothes and hotter exes. We watched as Carrie chose not to settle with any number of Mr. Wrongs, including Aidan, her Mr. Comfortable. Carrie struggled with the conflicts we all face: Do I want to get married? Do I want kids? How do you know when it's right? What's more important: the excitement of a bad boy or the comfort of a good guy? Carrie was Everywoman. She doubted her decisions, relied heavily on her friends, and sometimes made an ass of herself. The friendships among Carrie, Samantha, Miranda, and Charlotte were the most powerful aspect of the show. It tackled the fear of never finding that all-consuming love, the depression that hits when you realize you don't have anyone to help you zip up your dress, and the boredom of hanging out with a bunch of lo-bridemized friends in the 'burbs. The characters were strong, weak, and complicated.

Foe

Because it was such an amazing show that spoke to so many of us, it was that much more disappointing that, for all its celebration of singledom and female empowerment, it ended with everyone neatly coupled. Even oversexed, relationship-resistant Samantha, changed by cancer, settles down with her younger beau. Most atrocious of all, our heroine Carrie gets "rescued" by the jerk whose baggage she's been carrying like a pathetic porter for years. Is it any wonder that when *Sex and the*

City aired in Germany, the title was translated to *Finding a Husband*? Leave it to the Germans to cut to the quick.

Static Source: Chuck the Chick Lit

Welcome to chick lit, the ghetto of female-penned books where every cover features the lower half of a woman in pointy shoes carrying a shopping bag or a designer dog. We're all for the advancement of women writers, but really, why does every chick lit novel have the exact same plot?

We loved *Bridget Jones's Diary* because Bridget was an average, imperfect, neurotic woman who was always trying to lose five pounds and couldn't seem to get through a dinner party without somehow putting her foot in it. Finally, someone we could relate to, right? Well, except for the fact that she gets her happy ending, too. And for the fact that she spawned so many knockoffs. Let's just call them what they are: paperback rom coms. Same old story over and over again.

Tune it out: some female authors who will provide an escape from the Bridal Wave:*

1. *The Girl in the Flammable Skirt* by Aimee Bender
2. *Reading Lolita in Tehran* by Azar Nafisi
3. *Tiny Ladies in Shiny Pants* by Jill Soloway

*While Karen McCullah Lutz's *The Bachelorette Party* won't keep you out of the wedding world, it's still a hilarious read about the trauma of the Everyone-I-Know-Is-Getting-Married Years from the single chick's perspective.

4. *Slouching Towards Bethlehem* by Joan Didion
5. *It's My F—ing Birthday* by Merrill Markoe
6. *The Idiot Girl's Action-Adventure Club* by Laurie Notaro
7. *This Is Not Chick Lit,* edited by Elizabeth Merrick and featuring Francine Prose, Aimee Bender, Curtis Sittenfeld, Jennifer Egan, and Samantha Hunt
8. *The Time Traveler's Wife* by Audrey Niffenegger
9. *The Myth of You and Me* by Leah Stewart

Static Source: Romantic Comedies

Girl meets guy. Girl hates guy (and vice versa). Something happens to bring them together. They fall in love. They have a misunderstanding that leads to a breakup. Somehow they resolve the conflict. Girl and guy get back together and get either married or engaged. Sound familiar?

"Chick flicks" or "date movies" are almost always love stories. Scan the audience at any of these, and you'll find it filled with women on girls' night out or girls with their bummed-looking boyfriends. We know that dragging dudes to these films is a form of cruel and unusual punishment, yet we continue to inflict it and also make a habit of looking over at them to see if they are "getting it." Why do we keep shelling out our dough to see the same story over and over again? It's as though we were masochists, going to movies that remind us that we are alone, and even if we do have a guy, he would never stand outside of our window playing "In Your Eyes" on a boom box. Maybe it has a little something to do with feeding the fantasy that we were sold on the first time someone read us a fairy tale: we have to get our fix somewhere because real life doesn't play out like a "feel-good" rom com.

Harmless entertainment? We hope so. Look at the top five lessons learned from romantic comedies.

1. Love happens in a moment, and no one really minds it if you end up with your boyfriend's brother, because, you know, he's "the one." In this oeuvre of film even the most unacceptable behavior is acceptable so long as it's in the name of true love. Source: *The Family Stone.*
2. It's all right to screw someone over as long as she is uptight or somehow unlikable. Feel free to leave her at the altar; she's a bitch anyway. Source: *Four Weddings and a Funeral.*
3. If you think you hate him, he may be "the one." Source: *You've Got Mail.*
4. Hiring a hooker is a shortcut to finding your soul mate. Source: *The Wedding Date, Pretty Woman.*
5. There's always a gorgeous girl hiding behind glasses and bad clothes just waiting for the right guy to reveal her. Source: *She's All That.*

Turn down the static: a few of our favorite films that don't end in "I do."

1. **Thelma and Louise.** Two women on the run from the law rediscover their friendship and themselves along the way. Classic. And the Brad Pitt "Take me, break me, make me a man" scene ain't bad either.

2. ***D.E.B.S.*** Plaid-skirted schoolgirls are groomed by a secret government agency to become the newest members of an elite national defense group. Girl loses boy, girl gets girl, and together they save the day.

3. ***Boys on the Side.*** Girl road trip movie that is actually very sweet and a total weeper in the best way.

4. ***La Femme Nikita* (the original).** Convicted felon Nikita avoids jail by getting a new identity and stylishly training to be a top secret assassin.

5. ***Eternal Sunshine of the Spotless Mind.*** Finally, a movie about the breakup fantasy we've all had—erasing a bad relationship. The heartbreak in this film is more genuine than anything we've ever seen in a rom com.

6. ***Lost in Translation.*** Maybe this unconventional love story makes so much sense because a chick actually wrote it. Scarlett Johansson plays a newlywed who discovers that marriage hasn't made her happy. She does fall in love in a way, but the movie is way too smart to end in the bedroom.

7. ***Walking and Talking.*** Once you get past the early-nineties fashion missteps, Nicole Holofcener's still-relevant film is a genuine example of a friendship surviving the Bridal Wave minus the 2-D characters.

Static Source: Bridal Magazines and Their Offspring, the Wedding Binder

Believe It or Knot

Ladies in Waiting

Almost 43 percent of *Modern Bride*'s circulation comes from subscriptions. Who exactly are these subscribers? Are these all really newly engaged women? Or women who subscribe so they're ready to hit the ground running as soon as the ring is on their finger? Consider this: the median age of its readers is 29.4. Sounds like there could be some women out there on the edge of 30 who are laying the foundation for the "big day," possibly even before they've met their mate.

InStyle Weddings, Martha Stewart Weddings, TheKnot.com, *Elegant Bride, Modern Bride, Brides, Allure Bride.* The number and size of these magazines keep growing, and this just in: Fairchild Publications' *Brides* magazine is launching a second annual spin-off: *Bride's Honeymoons and Weddings Away,* "designed to tap into the market for destination weddings." How helpful, right?

Maríbel, twenty-five and single, told us that she has been reading bridal magazines for years. "If I'm bored and not doing anything, I'll go to Borders and flip through the bridal mags for an hour. I just do it to get ideas." Sounds lighthearted and innocent, right? Read on. "I'll buy a magazine every once in a while. It's fun for me, an indulgence. Where someone might go out and buy chocolates, I treat myself to bridal magazines." While we love her approach to saving calories and simultaneously getting a biceps workout (have you ever tried to lift one of those bridal mags?), Maríbel is not as casual as she sounds. She went on to tell us that she has "pretty much the entire ceremony planned out. Definitely a church wedding, and I have all of the music and scriptures picked out. Obviously there is room for flexibility, but there are things I know that I want. When I go to a wedding, I kind of scope out what the couple did, and then I'll go home and make notes of what I liked and what I didn't, so I make sure not to make the same mistakes the couple did. For example, I went to an outdoor wedding and it started to rain. It was obvious by how panicked everyone was that they had no Plan B. I will never make that mistake." Slow down there, partner. Having your wedding planned down to the boutonniere without having a boyfriend is setting yourself up for disappointment.

Maríbel is not alone. Meet the cult of the wedding binder. Women, some of whom are very single, pull pics of flowers they like, table settings that appeal to them, and other such persnickety points and put them away for safekeeping. Creating one of these won't get you any closer to getting married. In fact, it's like keeping a closet full of clothes that would fit if you lost ten pounds. And let's be practical: If you start your binder when you're twenty-two and get married when you're thirty-two, what good are those pics going to be? Can you say "outdated"?

Avoid the Noise

There is no way to completely pull the plug on pop culture, not when the home page of MSN is reporting on celebrity splits. Assuming you don't want to pack it in and build a shack in Montana, here are some ways you can avoid the matrimania without becoming a recluse or a killjoy:

- **Go where the boys are.** No, not so you can cruise them. Hanging out with guys can provide a well-needed respite from wedding static. Dudes don't discuss celebrity couplings or the latest tearjerker. Plus, if you go to see a sci-fi film with the guys, chances are the previews won't be for the soon-to-be-released rom com.

- **Tune in to your own reality.** Understand that what you are seeing on these "reality" shows is anything but reality. The celebrity profiles? Fiction.

- **Bottoms up.** Get some friends together and turn *The Bachelor,* or some such show, into a drinking game. Pick a phrase or word, and every time it is said, drink. For example, every time a contestant says that she feels a real "connection," take a sip of whatever makes you happy.

- **Stop flipping.** Watch the shows that you truly enjoy, but don't spend time flipping for something to watch. If you have a DVR, record only what you want to watch and watch only those shows. Spend the extra hours socializing with friends—not lobridemized ones.

- **Go beyond the style section.** Having a broader scope of the world around you will help shrink your wedding fears down to size. Plus, when you meet a guy, you'll have something to talk about besides the latest celeb breakup.

Repeat After Us

I understand that I am not a celebrity. Because I am not Tori Spelling, I understand that I will not have fireworks at my wedding, nor an ice sculpture of my fiancé. I also understand that having a wedding worthy of a magazine spread does not mean my marriage will work or that I will be happy. I know that despite my uncanny resemblance to a certain star, we actually have nothing in common, even if we have the same birthday and use the same face cream. I will broaden the range of books and magazines I read so I don't lock myself into a world run by the moneymaking celebrity machine that perpetuates happily-ever-after myths. If friends are talking about the latest wedding reality show, I promise to point out how weird it is that women are competing to marry the same guy, whom they hardly know. I will say with an air of indignation, "Don't these women understand that marriage is not a prize to be won?" Once in a while I will say no to paying ten bucks to see the most recent boy-meets-girl flick. I will take every opportunity to turn down the volume on the marriage static, and when it cannot be avoided, I will remind myself that sitcoms are written by a bunch of usually fat and pasty guys, romantic comedies and chick lit are fairy tales for adults, and the only reality I know is my own, so I'll spend the time making it more interesting than anything I could watch or read.

CHAPTER 7

Spinster City

**Will I die alone and be eaten by cats?
Our biggest fears about not finding a mate**

"I guess my biggest fear is that somehow something is wrong with me and all of my friends are just too nice to tell me what it is."

"If I turn thirty and still haven't even had a serious boyfriend, I'm going to be worried. I mean, outwardly, I'm fine and busy. But in the privacy of my own apartment, I've been known to sit on the couch and have a sob session out of loneliness and fear."

"I couldn't take being single anymore and finally signed up for an online dating service, only to be told there were no matches for me. Now what do I do?"

"I feel like the pity friend of my married friends. Like, they make a point of calling and inviting me out on weekends, because they assume if they don't I'll just sit at home depressed with Netflix and a big bag of Pirate's Booty."

"I have one other single friend left, and if she gets a boyfriend before me, I don't know how I'm going to deal. I know it's mean, but I'm counting on her being the last single one."

"When I saw my best friend walk down the aisle, I knew I was supposed to feel happy for her, but all I could think was 'Is this ever going to happen for me?' Isn't that terrible?"

"When I was twenty-five, I decided I would date a hundred people in a year in my search for 'the one.' I figured with numbers on my side, maybe I would be able to find one person who wanted similar things. It was exhausting and not fun at all. I want to get married so that I never have to date again!"

There's an elephant in the room, and we aren't talking about some unfortunate soul in a slate gray bridesmaid's dress. We're talking about the fear that grows larger with every passing year of the Bridal Wave, the fear at the other end of all the panic and pressure we endure: that if you don't find someone soon or at least get yourself on track, you're going to end up A-L-O-N-E. It's a big, bad subject, and in today's tell-all world, this is one thing we don't really talk about. We may happily chitchat with our close friends about terrible blind dates, what our therapist says, even our favorite sex position, but nothing stops a conversation like revealing your secret fear that you are never going to meet someone who loves you enough to marry you.

If you do fess up, your well-meaning friends tend to jump in with "Don't be silly!" or "Of course you'll find someone!" before changing the subject as quickly as possible. It's all too obvious that they don't *really* want to engage in this conversation, and it's understandable why they wouldn't. They love you and probably have no idea why you're single. (Or if they do, they may worry that it's not their place to tell you.) So we keep our worries to ourselves and let them out by watching a good tearjerker, having a breakdown, or holding a private pity party.

You don't have to be the girl caught up in the fairy-tale ideal of marriage to have a mortal terror about winding up as the decrepit old hag in the story instead of the lovely princess. We all have fears about ending up alone, and there's nothing more panic-inducing than seeing your friends take the plunge to make you feel like you're still in the kiddie pool. All right, ladies, take a deep breath and let's face this stuff head-on.

Getting an "F" in Adulthood

Today falling in love is the ultimate goal in life. It may seem that we have become slaves to consumerism, but in literature, film, and advertising, we are told over and over again that "love is all you need" (as long as we buy the right products to help us get it). And not just love, but "the one." What does it mean if we're still single by a certain age—are we somehow not marriage material? Are we never going to have a family of our own and move on to that next stage in life? Being picked last in gym class was bad enough, but at least then you knew it was because your hand-eye coordination left much to be desired.

Believe It or Knot

Our idea of a love marriage, of a couple looking into each other's eyes and realizing that "you were meant for me, and I was meant for you" didn't begin until around the middle of the nineteenth century. From a way to secure an inheritance to forging alliances between countries, marriage before that was anything but romantic.

It seems like even the biggest freaks you know are able to find someone to love them. But if you're always the sole singleton in your friendship circle, does it mean you suck at the game of life?

From Val

When I graduated from high school without ever having a date, let alone a boyfriend, I wasn't too bothered. The guys at my school sucked anyway. It wasn't like I suffered from unrequited love. I was moving to California for college and figured that I would start a whole new chapter of my life. When freshman year went by and I was not living the wild college life that you see in movies—heck, I still hadn't had a date—I began to worry. After college my dating status remained the same: nonexistent. Soon, every time one of my fellow single friends found a boyfriend—or worse, when a friend who had broken up with her guy was suddenly dating someone new—I found myself swallowing my loneliness and pushing it deeper inside myself. To say I was jealous would be too simple.

How I felt was worse than jealous; I felt defective in some way. "What is wrong with me?" and "Am I so bad?" I remember talking to Erin, who was lamenting the loss of a relationship. I told her that at least someone had loved her once and for that she was better off than me. She disagreed. She felt like the loss was worse. I can tell you, she was wrong. The old adage "Better to have loved and lost than never to have loved at all" speaks volumes. I felt like having lost in love gave Erin a stamp of worthiness—a validation. Never having had that feeling dredged up my worst fears: that something was inherently wrong with me, that I was somehow not doing something right. Either I had *missed out on some window of opportunity to get into the dating scene or I was walking around missing whatever it was that made guys ask girls out.*

From Erin

After you've spent a few years of your life with someone, growing into them, getting to know their family, losing all of that in one rip-your-heart-out breakup can be shattering. The loneliness you are suddenly thrust into is an entirely different kind of monster than the loneliness I knew before because I had never had a boyfriend. For one, it's very specific. It's not an ambiguous fear that you'll never find love, or the general aloneness you feel when the dreaded V-Day rears its red head of roses and chocolate and the last Valentine you remember getting was from your fifth-grade science partner. It's an ache for someone's voice, touch, and smell that have been a palpable part of your life. It's the constant replaying of the best and worst moments of your time together, like a sick torture film festival in your head. Plus, all of your routines are suddenly broken—if you always made Sunday brunch together and sat around reading the paper, you're going to feel like the loneliest girl in the world on that first Sunday sans your ex. That kind of alone makes you feel more vulnerable than anything. Heartbreak is no picnic. Telling yourself "At least I had a relationship once" is no consolation for the fact that all you want is that relationship back, no matter how terrible it was, and having to accept that it's never going to happen. I felt defective, too. Why couldn't I make it work?

There's a part of you that knows these feelings are irrational (that's why we don't say a lot of them out loud!). But irrational or not, they are totally normal. Our society tends to associate being married with being grown up. So we know there's this shame that despite graduating summa cum laude, you've failed some part of the program or missed the lecture on finding a partner. (Kind of funny when you think about twenty-two-year-old Britney Spears getting married in Vegas in ripped acid-washed jeans and getting the marriage annulled fifty-five hours later. Subsequently marrying K-Fed didn't help her case.) Getting married does not make you an adult. Period.

Forever the Odd (Wo)Man Out

Thirty-year-old Maria told us that when all your friends become wives and husbands, "you have no choice but to couple up by default or else it's Single Saturdays forever." Being single is fine when everyone else in your peer group is, too, but when they start decamping for the married side and "settling down," there are a lot more nights in, unless you want to find a whole new group of friends.

Members Only

Rosie told us, "My married friends don't invite me to some of their get-togethers. It's like some weird couples-only thing. They try to keep it all super hush-hush, but I always end up finding out when someone mentions a funny story from the other night and then all the marrieds give each other an 'Oh, crap' look, like they've just busted themselves. What the hell? Do they sit around and discuss how great it is to be married all night?" Sure, Rosie's friends have every right to choose whom they want to invite to their dinner parties, but not inviting someone because they aren't coupled up seems pretty lame to us. Then again, Rosie is certainly not going to meet the man of her dreams sitting around playing Trivial Pursuit with a bunch of couples.

Positive Polly would say, "Your friends don't want to make you feel well, 'singled' out by having you as the only unattached guest at the otherwise even numbered table. They're trying to spare you that record-scratch moment when everyone suddenly realizes that you've been silent for hours, leaving them to change the topic of conversation with about as much subtlety as Mariah Carey in *Glitter*. Sample conversation clunker:

Married Woman #1: We haven't finished all of our thank-you notes either! It's difficult to do, especially with my mother-in-law offering editorial comments on each note I send out!

Married Woman #2: (*laughing*) I know! I'm worried that as soon as I'm done with the notes she's going to get on me about having a baby!

Married Woman #3: Just wait until you've had your five-year anniversary! That's when the serious baby watch begins!

(*Awkward pause, worried glances*)

Married Woman #1: So, Janet, how is that sewing class you signed up for? Are you still taking that?

Janet: Yeah. I just made a skirt cut on the bias, which was a nightmare.

(Another awkward pause)
Married Woman #2: Oh, I know! My wedding dress was cut on the bias! Nightmare!

On the other hand, Negative Nell would see the members-only movement like this:

1. Your friends are enchanted with their own married status and think that it's very grown up to have a dinner party with their other married friends.
2. If the party is made up of a group of girlfriends with their spouses, it's probably an attempt to have the men bond. Think of it as a play date with cloth napkins.

How to handle feeling left in the dust socially

• **Be honest.** Tell your friend that you don't want her to feel obligated to invite you to her soirees, but you are feeling a bit left out. If she is empathetic and seems to "get it," leave it at that. If she becomes crazy-defensive or can't understand where you're coming from, she may be too self-centered to be worth the fight. If she puts in zero effort to maintain the friendship, maybe you should, too.

• **Throw a no-couples party.** Nothing makes a married person feel like a boring old married couple than not being invited to hang with singles. Invite your new friends (because of course you've been recruiting unwedded pals ever since we told you there's strength in numbers), and they'll bring other unattached friends.

The Most Dangerous Predator: The Single Woman

We jest, but there is something threatening about a single woman among a group of marrieds. Don't be surprised if you become enemy number one of your desperate housewife acquaintances, particularly the wives of your male buds. It totally blows, but during the Bridal Wave years a single gal tends to lose a lot of her male friends. Sherri, twenty-seven, was a bit of a guy's girl. She always had more male friends than female, and she noticed that as soon as they popped the question to their girlfriends they also stopped calling Sherri to hang out. One guy in particular, Josh, actually told her what was going on. "My wife thinks you have a crush on me, so she has asked me to stop seeing you," he said. Sherri was horrified. She had never even considered Josh in any way other than a fellow *Star Wars* nerd, and now she was losing a friend because of his wife's jealousy. In an attempt to keep the friendship going, Sherri had Josh and his wife over for dinner. It was tense and filled with long lulls in conversation. Sherri chalked it up to the inherently uncomfortable situation of knowing that you are being watched for any signs of a crush. Josh's wife attributed the dud night to Sherri having to suppress her crush. Sherri decided that if Josh's wife didn't trust him enough to hang out with her, she would end the friendship rather than be blamed for any marital problems down the road. Bummer that she lost a friend, but not that she lost the drama.

The Vacation Conundrum

Being a party of one also poses a challenge when it comes to vacations. If you've got wanderlust, it isn't always that fun (or safe) to travel on your own, and of course your coupled friends are always going to go with their partners. So what's a girl to do?

• Visit far-off friends. Reconnect with your first roommate in college, or claim that's what you want to do when you ask if you can stay at her place in London while you explore the city. Having a local as a tour guide is the best way to really get the feel of a city and save a ton on lodging. If your friends have moved but not to anywhere you'd want to visit, you may want to . . .

• Seek out new friendships with other single girls who might make good traveling mates. Don't want to make new friends? You could . . .

• Organize an annual girls' weekend and convince your married friends to ditch their other halves for a long weekend. Chances are, they'll relish the thought of reliving (some of) their single ways. Over time friends tend to drift apart. Having an annual date is a great way to stay connected.

• Get to know the woman who is your mother. Okay, this may sound depressing, but traveling with your mother when you are an adult can be a wonderful experience. She doesn't have to worry about you falling into the Trevi Fountain anymore, and when she asks strangers to take a photo of you two, you won't turn crimson with embarrassment and pretend like you have no idea who she is. If Mom has no desire to leave home . . .

- Book yourself on an organized trip with like-minded travelers. Don't scoff! The Sierra Club (www.sierraclub.org), for example, offers backpacking, biking, camping, canoeing, kayaking, sailing, skiing, and more.

Whatever you do, find a way to take a vacation. A study by Expedia.com found that employees are handing companies more than $21 billion in unused vacation days each year.[1] You earn those vacation hours; use them! Not having a boyfriend or a husband is no excuse.

I'll Never Have a Family of My Own

The itch to hitch can be fierce if you want to have kids someday, because we're told it goes like this: first comes love, then comes marriage, then comes baby in the baby carriage. The thirty-five-year-old time bomb has been ticking in our heads for years. We fear that not meeting Mr. Right by thirty means we'll be childless. We imagine holidays where we're forever a guest in someone else's house or always someone's "aunt" even when we share no blood ties. And in 2002 the headlines started flying around that a woman's fertility actually began to decrease at twenty-seven.[2] That helpful info detonated fear for a whole new legion of women in their mid-twenties!

Let's get some perspective: "begins to decrease" *does not mean "drops significantly."* While a woman born in 1900 could expect to live until she was fifty-one years old, a woman born in 1980 can expect to see her seventy-seventh birthday.[3] We need to re-align our timelines. These days, having a baby when you're forty is far from unheard of. The bottom line: if you want to have a family someday (and even if you aren't so sure) the best thing you can do for yourself during the Bridal Wave years is to *stay healthy and strong:*

1. Quit smoking now, even if you have only one or two cigarettes when you go out.
2. Get calcium to those bones, whether it is from milk, cheese, yogurt, or a daily supplement.
3. Start a regular exercise program.

Take these measures so that when you are ready to raise a little one, your body will be up to the task. Have you tried carrying a baby and all the paraphernalia that is needed to keep them occupied/dry recently? The word "sciatica" comes to mind.

Of course, the latest news is all about women who are adopting from abroad or using a sperm donor. People love to squawk about the quiet desperation of these women or use it as a "See what happens when you hit the snooze button one too many times on the ol' biological clock alarm?" moral, but for many women who know they want to be a mom, it's simply a matter of making sure that happens, whether they find Mr. Right or not.

Single Mom by Choice

Jennifer, thirty-two, never thought she'd be single. "I was perpetually in relationships since I was fourteen, but since my last five-year relationship ended, I've had a three-year drought. In that time, I finished my postdoc, opened my own practice, and bought a house. I've gone from enjoying my friends' babies but being glad to say good-bye to them to wanting my own pretty fast. Careerwise I've gotten very stable, even though my relationships are topsy-turvy. So I've started talking to everyone about using a sperm donor to conceive a child because I didn't want anyone to fall off their chairs if I was pregnant soon with no guy in sight. They all say, 'You still have time,' and I know that. I would love to meet someone. I'm out there, but I'm not going to just settle for any person. Even if on paper they are smart choices, treat me well, and would make great fathers, I can't do it if it's not authentic. I'm not waiting on any man to decide what I'm doing. It's not who I am. It doesn't mean I have to give up my search for someone to share my life with. It just means I know I want to be a mom and I will be."

Maybe it's no one's fantasy to drive to a sperm bank and play select-a-dad. But if your biggest fear of never marrying is that you'll never have kids, then you need to realize that you don't *have* to get married to achieve that. Opting to have a baby on your own doesn't mean the end of the line for you romantically. They can be separate things. It is 2007, after all! We know being a single mom is tough, but even if you tie the knot, it's no guarantee that your guy is going to stick around to change diapers and be the dad of your dreams. If you're whining about wanting babies, do something about it. Offer to be the babysitter for your friends so you get a real taste of the demands. If that doesn't scare you off, investigate adoption or sperm donation. That's a better use of your time than running out of someone's baby shower in tears at the sight of the stroller.

I Don't Want to End Up Like Her

Everybody seems to have a spinster relative somewhere in the family or a middle-aged woman in her office who is single and just seems *sooo* sad and alone. "I read my family history once, and all it said for one woman was 'Eva Bates, died fifty-two years old.' And I thought, *What did this woman do for fifty-two years?*" recalls Jill. "They only wrote a real entry for women if they were married and had children. For a while, I was really freaked that my place in the family tree would read the same: my name, followed by how old I was when I died a spinster in New York City."

Towanna, twenty-nine, has a long-term boyfriend but no desire to wed. She is happy with her life and her independence and doesn't see children in her future. Towanna's co-workers love to needle her about her position on marriage: "You're gonna lose that man when he moves on to someone who wants the family thing." They even throw out this zinger: "Do you want to end up like Lorelai?" Frankly, *no,* Towanna does *not* want to end up like Lorelai, who is in her fifties, never married, and the embodiment of the word "mousy." Even though she knows she is nothing like Lorelai, their catty comments can get to her. *Is* her boyfriend going to leave her for someone more "traditional"?* Is Towanna going to be the Lorelai of future cautionary tales? Of course, what *seems* to be and what *is* are often two different stories. Lisa's Great-aunt Goldie lived alone in Brooklyn. She worked as a high school math teacher, and for years Lisa felt sorry for her. "I thought she was the only sister who had never gotten married—and that she must be so disappointed with her life." Then she found out the true story: Goldie had been married once to a guy who didn't want kids. Goldie had always wanted children. So she divorced him. She never remarried and never had kids but still never regretted her decision. She was active in her community, volunteered for many cool organizations, and whenever she had a spare moment, she painted.

People love to say things like "Why aren't you out there? Do you want to wind up like Aunt Goldie?" Or "Look at Bette. Sure, she made partner, but she's got no one to share it with. Her life must be so empty. Maybe you should say yes to him." The truth is, some women who end up alone have done so by choice and revel in their decision. Just goes to show that you can't judge a woman's happiness by her honorific. And you certainly can't let bored co-workers influence how you live your life.

*If he does, then good riddance; he wasn't the right guy for her anyway.

Believe It or Knot

When we lived in Japan, some of our friends told us that single women after the ripe old age of twenty-five (and this from a country whose average life span for women is eighty-two years—the longest life expectancy in the world) are called "Christmas cake." In Japan the Christmas cake is traditionally eaten on Christmas Eve, so this expression conveys the idea that women over twenty-five are undesirable marriage partners, as unwanted as day-old sponge cake, to be exact. Interestingly, according to our unscientific sources, more women were offended by the "stale" connotation than by being compared to cake in the first place.

Am I Failing as a Feminist If I Want a Ring?

There aren't many people who would prefer a lifetime of solitude versus growing old with someone who promises to love you even if your teeth fall out. Still, admitting that we want to get married is difficult for some of us. Women have fought against the whole "need a man" thing for years, so it's easy to feel guilty or even ashamed about our wish to wed. We get MBAs now, not MRSs. Are we traitors to the cause if we secretly yearn to have a husband and be a wife? Marriage is still caught up with "girly" notions a lot of us have a hard time stomaching.

It's completely normal to want to share your life with some-one. But obsessing over something you can't control or pre-dict, or compromising your standards for fear you won't find anyone else, is unhealthy.

 ————————————————

ARE YOU AS INDEPENDENT AS YOU THINK?

1. You're meeting a friend for dinner at 7:30 P.M. At 7:45, there's no sign of her and she's not answering her phone. What do you do?
   a. Sidle up to the bar or ask to be seated at your table, and order your favorite drink while you wait.
   b. Glance around the room and start mentally calculating all the happy coupled-up people. Start feeling sorry for yourself. If she's not there in three minutes, you're bailing and sending her an angry text.
   c. Sit at the bar but put your phone out and check it every two minutes. Um, clearly you aren't alone on a prime date night.

2. You've been seeing a guy for a few months, but, let's face it, he's fun to be with and not bad to look at, but you're just not that into him. A friend of yours from work has been raving

about this new guy her hubby works with she thinks is just perfect for you. When do you cut and run from guy number one?

  a. As soon as you realize it isn't going to go anywhere. Why waste your (and his) time?

  b. After you've gone on a couple of dates with Mr. New. That way, you can strategically segue from Saturday nights with Mr. So-So to Saturday nights with Mr. New without any stopover in Singleville. You may not have had a real boyfriend in three years, but no one can really call you single, either.

  c. You mean Backup Bob? Why send off a Just-in-Case you've been simmering to perfection on the back burner? Until Prince Charming shows up (and you'll know it when you see that white horse), you're keeping him around.

3. It's a Friday night, and you have no plans. Your go-to girls are either out of town, down with the flu, or ugh, happily ensconced in a new relationship. What do you do with the blank spot in your diary?

  a. Make it a blockbuster night! You hit the gym for the spin class you really like but can never make, then pick up wine, a movie, and your favorite takeout and relish the night in alone.

  b. Call Mr. Platonic Pal, the straight guy who's not so secretly in love with you and who'll drop anything to hang with you when you call. You hit the grocery store with him and buy food to make for dinner. It's just like you're a couple, except for you're not.

c. Change into something fabulous at work and prep in the bathroom with all the other girls, gabbing about the surprise date this new guy has planned for you. Then you head...straight home, where you cry your eyes out about being single while inhaling all the junk food you can find. After your snack attack, you shed new tears about how you're too fat to find love.

If you answered **mostly A's,** you're our kind of girl. Sure, it'd be nice to have a boyfriend, but you enjoy your time too much to waste it on some loser you don't like.

If you answered **mostly B's,** you're fooling yourself with your independent act. You may not have a real BF, but you've set up training wheels to ensure you're never really flying solo. Time to let go and take a spin—even if you fall.

If you answered **mostly C's,** you're missing out on getting to know someone who's really cool—yourself—because you're afraid of what other people think. And do we have to remind you that pretending that you aren't alone when you are is not exactly the best way to meet someone?

Learning to be comfortable in any situation is one of the most important things to do for yourself. Knowing you can rely on yourself will free you to take risks, speak your mind, and be honest with your feelings. And bravado is a wicked turn-on. Women like Oprah, Madonna, Angelina, and Danica Patrick would never have gotten very far if they had been worried about what other people thought of them.

Strategies for When We're Feeling Low

To help herself deal with the "Oh my God, everyone I know is getting married, what the hell is wrong with me?" feeling, Barbara said, "The most reassuring revelation I had being single and fearing the lack of control—that I was never going to find this person—was just to allow myself to think that this person exists, he's actually living and breathing somewhere. I started picturing him, nothing specifically, maybe he's reading a book or going to a concert. I didn't give him a name or a height or hair color. But at times when I was freaking out that I would never get married, I was like 'Hmm, maybe he's at IKEA.' It was really comforting. When you realize this person exists, it alleviates the fear of if you're ever going to meet someone. People find each other, and right now he's hanging out somewhere, and soon our paths will cross."

Don't panic! Instead of freaking out about being single:

- **Exercise.** Getting to the gym is a hurdle, but you know you'll feel better when the endorphins kick in. Your mind will be clearer, your face will have a nice glow, and you'll have done something good for yourself.

- **Channel your inner seven-year-old.** What did you love to do when you were a kid? Paint watercolors? Play soccer? Collect rocks? We spend so much of our lives either working or being passively entertained that we forget we were once thrilled about jumping in a big pile of leaves.

- **Dance it out.** Close the curtains, turn down the lights, turn up the music, and dance like an idiot in front of a mirror. Go on, grab a hairbrush and sing along. There is no way to be bummed when you are invoking classic, pre-Nipplegate Janet. (Ms. Jackson, if you're nasty.)

- **Document it.** Writing about how you really feel with the knowledge that nobody will ever read your words can be incredibly cathartic. The best part? No more younger sibs sneaking into your room and reading your diary aloud at the dinner table!

- **Reach out and touch someone.** Not that kind of touching. We mean call a friend. They don't call it a buddy system for nothing. Keep the Bridal Wave worries from boiling over.

- **Challenge yourself.** For some of us, that could mean taking a public speaking course; for others that could mean BASE jumping. Doing something that scares you will remind you that life is to be lived to the fullest and "to the fullest" does not require matching pots and pans.

- **Call it a wash.** Sometimes it's the struggle that makes us so miserable. Every now and then, go with the undertow. Everybody is going to have these feelings at some point. Let them wash over you, and they'll pass.

Embrace Your Single Self

For most of our adolescence we want to be older than we are: We buy *Seventeen* magazine when we're twelve, finagle fake IDs so we can get into twenty-one-and-over clubs when we're seventeen. Once we're in high school, we want to skip on ahead to college (and college boys). Rarely do we sit back and enjoy where we are *right now*. Our twenties and thirties are a time of getting to know ourselves, but just when we are figuring out how to live on our own as adults, our friends start talking about cake-cutting fees and our family begins to question our lack of the ultimate accessory: a husband. Great. How can you feel good about where you are?

Here's the thing: your single days are numbered, and once they're gone, they're gone (barring a divorce, which you smart readers will avoid, having read this book).

What you'll miss about being single
1. Take it from the late, great Kate (Hepburn): "If you want to sacrifice the admiration of many men for the criticism of one, go ahead, get married."
2. Going to the gym whenever you want, even at midnight. Nobody is waiting for you to get home.
3. Eating chips and salsa for dinner. Getting married does not a gourmet make, but busting out the chips and salsa for dinner doesn't really work for a guy.
4. Plucking your eyebrows for hours on end without someone asking what the heck is going on in there.
5. Going out after work with friends without having to call

home to "check in." A wedding band doesn't mean you'll never go out for happy hour, but it does mean calling to make sure it's cool with your hubby (in an evolved, non-permission-slip-type way).

The grass is always greener (admissions from anonymous married women)

"If I were single again, I would really learn how to flirt. I feel like I got married before I really grew into my body. I would love to go out and really go for it."

"Sure, I love my husband, but sometimes I wish I could blink my eyes and he would be gone. I don't want him to die, I just want him to not exist for a little so I could be single again and just worry about myself."

"I was so worried about never getting married that I married the first guy who showed interest in me. We're happy together, but I wonder if I had just waited a bit longer, where would I be today?"

Why being unmarried rocks

1. You aren't in an unhappy marriage. We repeat: you aren't in an unhappy marriage. Married couples may seem like they have it all, but you have no idea what happens behind closed doors.

2. You can do what you want when you want. Feel like leaving a papier-mâché project unfinished on the dining table? Do it. Want to watch an entire season of *Grey's Anatomy* in one sitting? Do it!

3. You never know when or where you are going to meet the next guy you'll fall madly in love (or lust) with, so every day is another day that it could happen. That's pretty cool.

4. A first date doesn't pee with the bathroom door open. (If he does, head for the hills!)

5. You have more time to hang with all of your obnoxious girlfriends—you know, the ones your boyfriends never like but you think are hilarious.

6. No in-laws. 'Nuff said.

7. Hookups! You can flirt the night away with a guy just for fun even if you have no interest in him. You can even make out with him.

8. All of your hard-earned cash can be spent on priority number one: you.

9. No stinky man laundry.

10. You can move to another city just because you like its name without having to worry about whether or not he wants to go or if he'll be able to find a job.

Sanity-Saving Vows

Repeat After Us

I promise not to grade myself based on whether or not I have said "I do."
I know that while falling in love is great, it is not as easy as buying the right perfume/cosmetic/weight-loss product, though billions of dollars are spent trying to make me believe

it is. I won't be bummed about not getting invited to the smug married dinner club because I will be out on the town with my new fabulous single friends. I will stop making lists of male friends with good genetic attributes who could be potential sperm donors because I'm twenty-eight and nowhere near tying the knot. I will relish my complete liberty and my ability to join the circus in New Zealand if I see fit because I don't have to factor someone else into my decision. I will spend more time doing things that make me feel proud of my independence and competence so that I never "need" a man but I won't beat myself up for wanting one. *I know that calling on my gay husbands to play switch-hitter when I need male stand-ins doesn't exactly help my case of seeming available. When I get really down about being alone, I will remember that the first 120 days of a new relationship are full of lust, excitement, and sweetness and I still have another 120 days to look forward to. I realize that there are a ton of married women who would kill to be as free and breezy as I am. So for all of them, I am going to live it up and do my best to justify their jealousy. I won't put up an inspirational poster by my desk or anything, but I will live every day as if it's my last single one.*

CHAPTER 8

A Shoulder to Lean On, Not a Bank Account to Sponge Off

Looking for a way out of debt and that crappy studio? Get a raise, not a husband

The Best Years of Your Life?

Everyone wants to be in their mid-twenties. When you're a teenager, you crave independence and when you're old and gray, you miss your carefree ways. The beauty of being a young adult is the ability to do whatever you want whenever you want. Should be the time of your life, right? The problem is, you're twenty-five, so chances are your salary is about the same as the price of a Toyota Camry. That first paycheck can be a bit of shock. You don't have cash for what you want and what you need, let alone for attending your friend's wedding in Jamaica. You aren't even contributing to a 401(k), and your paycheck barely covers your rent. You have more expenses than ever before (car payment, anyone?), and suddenly you are hit by the Bridal Wave. You want to attend all of your friends' weddings, but at the same time you would also like to eat.

Imagine if the folks in our life who feel it necessary to question our romantic status felt as comfortable asking about our fiscal prospects. "So, how's that nice investment portfolio of yours?" "Do you think that you'll be next to buy?" Sure, it would be awkward, but at least you could answer those questions and possibly even glean some helpful information from their tips. Grandma's "Put on some rouge, dear, men don't want a plain Jane" likely goes in one ear and out the other, but her tip to "Always sock away a little money from each paycheck, so that when you need a little extra, you have it ready" could take up residence in your long-term memory. But instead, our savings accounts (or lack thereof) are the unmentionables.

If Grandma were really tuned in, she would know that how you handle yourself financially absolutely factors into your relationships. While most men don't have "Must have a perfect credit rating" at the top of their most wanted in a mate list, there is nothing sexy about signing on to someone else's debt or a woman who can't keep her finances in order. It may seem like no big deal when you pay your credit card late, but little slips like that stick around for quite some time (seven years, to be exact) and could affect your ability to get approved for a mortgage, a car loan, or even an apartment. Imagine if you met a guy who was great in every way except for his $20,000 of debt on his credit card from living the high life in his early twenties. You can deal with his snoring, but are you ready to pay (literally) for his past mistakes?

From Val

Like a lot of women, I graduated from college with credit card debt. I got into it a little at a time. I was the girl who would take your cash at dinner, pay the whole bill with plastic, and then spend the cash on something else. I never gave much thought to how long I would be paying for those dinners, lip glosses, shoes, and drinks. I thought that once I got a full-time job I would be able to pay it off. Then I got my piddly first paycheck and realized my debt wasn't going anywhere anytime soon. Not that I stopped charging, mind you. I optimistically assumed I was living the lifestyle that I would be able to afford when I got a better salary. Creditors loved me. I paid on time every month—the minimum due, that is—which meant that I was barely making a dent in the principle. As I reached the upper levels of my credit limits, those friendly folks would up my limit and my APRs. So thank you, Citibank, for those inspirational billboards about money not being everything in life, though I have a feeling that you were the ones "living richly" off of my debt.

When I started dating Tommy, I was blown away by the fact that he had no debt—or credit cards! How did he live? I came to find out that he saved a good portion of his paycheck and never dipped into the well for such "necessities" as lunches out every day or chichi brunches with his friends. When we started to get serious, I knew that I had to come clean with him about my debt. I was ashamed to tell him just how bad it was. I felt like I lost some IQ points with him that day. Here I was, an educated woman, still paying off dinners and totally out-of-style clothes from five years ago! Luckily, it wasn't a deal breaker, though we did have some *"talks" about money and about using credit cards—or, to be more exact, not using credit cards. Getting married means signing on to each other's financial past. Your debt becomes his debt, and vice versa. It does not feel good to be the one responsible for your first few years of marriage being dedicated to paying down debt.*

When we're unmarried, we have nobody to take care of but ourselves, yet we interpret taking care of ourselves to mean weekly mani/pedis and spending ridiculous sums of money on denim—a fabric that used to be worn to herd cattle. We don't want you to be the mousy sad girl who wears sensible shoes and eats strange-smelling leftovers alone at her desk. You should be your fabulous self. You should have fun and go out. But you shouldn't be doing it at the expense of setting yourself up for the future. We're too hung up on the fantasy of the salary that we will earn someday and having the two-person dual-income package deal that will grant instant financial security and some prefab notion of marital bliss. Or maybe we're waiting for that perfect combination of nice eyes, sensitive soul, and fat wallet. Hey, we like that picture too, but being self-sufficient doesn't mean you can't end up with that. It means you're always going to be able to take care of the most important person in your life: you.

Be honest, how much time did you spend choosing your 401(k)? How about investigating savings accounts? Okay, now how much time do you spend thinking about something you want to buy? How many conversations with your friends have you had about how to best invest your money versus whether or not the boho look will last beyond next season? There are the stellar exceptions like our friend Megan, who has managed to save over $15,000 while still maxing out her 401(k) with a salary *well under* the six-figure mark—in Manhattan, no less! When we asked her how she did it, she replied, "I buy my jeans at the Gap and my purses on the street." She thinks that most of her friends are broke because they are spending all their hard-earned money on trends. Why is it that we are so gung ho to move out on our own and live like adults, yet when it comes to dollars we seem to be missing some common cents?

Unwittingly, a lot of us play right into the stereotypes about women and money, because we're spending the energy (and the dough) on the find-a-man plan and its "necessary" accouterments. The funny thing is, not only do guys not care if you are wearing the latest and greatest brand of jeans, they would rather you be slightly out of style (which they wouldn't notice anyway) and not in debt because of a full closet. Guys are interested in what's underneath your clothes, and we don't mean your kindhearted personality. Bill, thirty-three, says, "Girls dress to impress each other, not guys. As long as your clothes look good on you, that's enough for us. We spend most of the night thinking about what's going on under your clothes anyway. A lot of girls buy what's 'in' but not what looks good on them. That goes for makeup, too."

Not being able to help pay for a vacation because you have maxed out your credit cards or complaining about your debt throughout dinner with your guy is not only annoying, it's a turnoff.

If your guy is superconcerned with your personal style, it could be a warning sign that he is looking for a mannequin, not a woman.

Saving Money in Style

Trying to save money is tougher when you're single. Ashley was lamenting her growing credit card debt yet felt like she had to keep spending money in order to have a social life and possibly meet a guy. "I need to go shopping so that I can have going-out clothes," she explained. "I can't keep wearing the same stuff year after year. And if I don't go out to a bar or restaurant, then where am I going to meet people?" What you need is to find a balance in your life between being in style and being a slave to *InStyle.* It's time to cut the cord with your therapist—your retail therapist, that is.

- **Repeat after us: "I can't afford those."** Learn the difference between instant gratification and self-satisfaction.

- **Spend on staples.** Ask yourself whether what you are about to purchase can be found on a "what's hot" list in some magazine. If it's "in" this season, chances are it's going to be "out" next season. If you can't see yourself wearing that bubble skirt a year from now, go find a knockoff. That way, when everyone else realizes they are as flattering as elasticized garbage bags, at least you haven't paid couture prices. Before splurging on the real deal, do a cost-benefit analysis.

• **Go vintage.** If you live in a major metropolitan area, your local Salvation Army may be cleared out of the good stuff, but vintage boutiques are still cheaper than traditional clothing stores. Not only will you save your dough, you won't run into someone wearing the exact same Banana Republic outfit as you.

• **Cool off.** Institute a mandatory twenty-four-hour waiting period before making a major purchase. You'd be surprised by how many things will slip your mind given some distance. You'll save not only money but also buyer's guilt and possibly some tough returns.

• **Buyer beware.** Know the return policy before the sale is final. Stores are getting tighter and tighter on their return policies.

• **The sales trap.** Just because those $500 shoes are now only $200 does not mean that you should buy them. We get sucked into a "good" deal. Sample sales are especially dangerous. The discount high tends to obscure the fact that we are about to buy a bright yellow, see-through tank top in the middle of January. Sure, it's from a designer you love, but a $50 tank top, while better than a $100 tank top, is not as good as no tank top at all or a $10 Old Navy tank top that you might actually wear.

Going Out Without Going Broke

When you're single, the idea of staying in and watching TV can make you feel desperate and deprived—like you're the last woman standing (or sitting, as it were). But spending a fortune on going out in the hopes of snagging a sugar daddy isn't a smart strategy. Here are some tips for living the good life without looking like the Queen of Cheap:

- **Cop out of cover charges:** Covers are for losers. Refuse to pay on principle. Why would you want to go somewhere where you have to spend money just to get in? Simply sniff and say, "Daahling, I don't pay covers."

- **Pull a switcheroo:** Switch between clear liquors and 7 UP or club soda. They look the same, but you'll have a cheaper bill and fewer hangovers.

- **Pay with the presidents.** For some reason, when we pay with credit cards we tend to tip 20 percent on drinks like we've had a meal, but when we pay with cash we tip somewhere around $1 per drink. We have no idea how the math works, but paying with cash always feels cheaper.

- **Dive in.** Pick a less scene-y bar and make it your place. Once you pay $2.50 for a beer, you will be hard pressed to drop $8 on the same beer at the bar of the moment, and your friends will think you're a trailblazer. (That is, until your dive bar becomes hip and starts charging eight bucks a beer.)

- **Dine at Chez Vous.** Meet for drinks or dinner, but not drinks *and* dinner. Have dinner at your house or at a friend's, then spend the cash on drinks. Eating at home will save you cash *and* calories. Plus, you can brush before hitting the bars with a pine nut wedged in your teeth.

- **BYO.** Many restaurants have a "bring your own" alcohol policy, and some don't even charge a corkage fee. How many times have you loved a $30 bottle of wine at a restaurant only to find it for $8.99 at your local wine shop? Even with an $8 corkage fee, you would come out ahead of the game. You may even score some points for looking like you know your vino.

- **Make friends with the staff.** Penny, twenty-five, loves being a regular. She makes it a point to frequent a few places that she enjoys and where she gets to know the employees. She sits at a counter or bar whenever one is available. By knowing the staff, she feels comfortable cruising in for a meal or drink alone because she has people to talk to. Also, every now and then someone will slip her a cocktail or dessert on the house.

- **Crash art openings.** Get dressed up and hit some galleries. They tend to have free wine and cheese, as well as plenty of interesting people who share your love of art—or at least your love of free wine and cheese.

- **Pitch in.** Volunteer for a cause. Work with Habitat for Humanity and spend a weekend building a home. You'll be off that couch, helping a family in need, and using power tools. How cool is that? Another idea: If you're a dog lover, head to your local shelter and volunteer to walk dogs for a few hours. You'll make a pooch's day.

- **Brown-bag it.** Seriously, girls, we know how hard it is to make a salad that tastes like a restaurant salad (why, oh why, is that?), but buying lunch every day and takeout for dinner really adds up. Make plans to have lunch with a friend in various public locales (a lot of swanky buildings in cities have lovely lobbies that you can chill in), but bring your eats. If you have a regular group of lunch pals, see if you can rotate lunch duty. That way, you'll probably have more inspired meals than the two pieces of bread you slapped together with some cheese before you dashed out the door.

- **Drip, please.** We all love to go out for coffee, and we all know that our daily $3.50 latte habit is an extravagance that we could easily do without. But here's a tip: Order a drip coffee instead. You get the coffeehouse experience without the coffeehouse expense. A drip usually comes in under a dollar, and you can add the free milk and sugar to your heart's content. Two added bonuses? One: No waiting for the barista to make the ten specialty drinks ahead of yours. Two: You'll make your friends' abbreviation-heavy (half caff, extra wet) orders sound amateurish and high maintenance. If you can't handle coffee without the foam, go for a hot tea. You'll save the same money and still make the other orders sound bourgeois.

A Tale of Woe: Don't Be a Denim Addict

Alex, twenty-five, moved back in with her parents because she felt it was a waste of her crappy salary to be paying rent when she still ate at and brought her laundry to her folks' house. So she ditched her pad and moved in with Mom and Dad. Unfortunately, Alex saw this as an opportunity to use her hard-earned cash on the important things in life, like $200 jeans to feed her self-diagnosed denim habit. Every month half of her salary automatically goes into a savings account, which is great except that she drains it regularly on going out and clothes to wear when going out. Alex is embarrassed to tell people that yes, she lives at home and no, she is not saving any money or working toward something impressive, like owning her own place. Alex is wasting an amazing chance to save her dough, buy a place, and get ahead of most of her friends. Sure, she's dressed really, really well, but at the end of the day, she's pulling off her designer duds in her old bedroom, decorated with horse statues and Barbie dolls. And what do you think a guy will remember more: her Henry Duarte custom-made boot-cut jeans or the fact that he had to pick her up at her parents'?

What's Your Spending Style?

We all like to think that we have our own style. We are unique. But when it comes to money, most of us fall into one of five categories. Which are you?

1. *The Live-for-Today Girl*
   - You do not have a savings plan because you live from paycheck to paycheck (and from minimum payment due to minimum payment due).

   - To buy things like airplane tickets, wedding presents, or even $5 of gas, you whip out the plastic, because not having money in your checking account is not going to stop you.

   - You're done spending when you can no longer go to the ATM because you have less than $20 in your account and you can take out money only in $20 increments.

   - You continue to shop because you work hard and you deserve it and really, you need to.

2. *The '49er, AKA the Gold Digger*
   - You don't have a savings plan because you are "investing" your money on yourself so you can attract a "quality" (i.e., at least six figures) man who will take care of you.

   - You know at least three places to meet a rich man.

- You believe that money can't buy love, but it can sure buy a lot of other nice things.

3. *The I'm-Just-Working-Until-I-Get-Married Girl*
- Staying at home is your idea of heaven.

- When the going gets tough at work, you think to yourself that someday you will be free from all this stress.

- Who cares if you never really get into the field you majored in? You don't plan on working too much longer anyway.

4. *The Stop-Here-Add-Spouse Girl*
You have a savings plan and are doing fine for yourself but continue to rent because
- Buying is something that couples do.

- If you buy a place, you may seem too successful to any potential suitors and you have been called "intimidating" in the past.

- If you buy a place, you are accepting the fact that you are alone.

5. *I Am Woman, Hear Me Roar*
- Not only do you have a savings account, you know the interest it earns.

- When you hear a woman complain about how she is always broke, you want to yell, "Maybe if you weren't spending all your money on Miu Miu bags you would have some cash in the bank!"

• You read about the aforementioned four types of women and thought to yourself, "Really? Are there really women out there like that?"

1. The Live-for-Today Girl

If this sounds like you, you're in good company. According to the Women's Institute for a Secure Retirement, women are more likely to carry credit card debt than men. Also telling is the fact that 54 percent of women in their twenties and thirties are more likely to acquire thirty pairs of shoes before saving $30,000 in retirement assets.[1] Remember that *Sex and the City* episode where Carrie realizes she's spent the equivalent of a down payment on an apartment on shoes? She was able to buy the apartment only after Charlotte donated the diamond engagement ring her ex-husband with the porn and performance problem gave her. Aside from getting better at negotiating, we can't do much about the fact that women continue to earn less than their male counterparts—76 cents for every $1[2] (for full-time, year-round employees)—but we *can* do something about the fact that women still lag behind men in planning for the future. After all, if there's one thing we hope we've taught you, it's that panicking during the Bridal Wave years isn't going to help you find a guy any faster. Some things are not in our control— so it's just smarter to focus on the things that are.

If you subscribe to the "but in a few years I will be making enough money to pay off this debt" philosophy, listen up: "someday" is not a financial plan. Amanda, twenty-five and one step above an entry-level salary, told us, "I was shocked when my boss told me that she had to postdate a $40 check until payday because it would bounce. I knew for a fact that her salary was in the six figures, and it wasn't like she was jetting off to the Swiss Alps at a moment's notice. Isn't the point of rising up the corporate ladder that you don't have to be biting your nails until the next payroll deposit? She told me something totally depressing: no matter how much money you make it will never seem like enough, because as soon as you have more money, you just start spending more. You trade in your economy car for a luxury SUV, you buy a bigger house—always something just out of your reach." You may not add to your debt, but a salary jump doesn't mean shop till you drop. *Live on what you make, not what you plan on making.*

Getting your financial house in order

If your monthly budget is "as long as I can still withdraw from the ATM, things are fine," it's time to change your ways. Hit the bookstore or, better yet, the library and head to the personal finance section. There are myriad books that can guide you toward getting control of your finances.

Hit the books

You aren't the only one struggling to make ends meet. New books like *Generation Debt* by Anya Kamenetz and *Strapped: Why America's 20- and 30-Somethings Can't Get Ahead* by Tamara Draut offer a window into the economic hardships facing those of us in our twenties and early thirties who are struggling to eke out a living. Both are heavy on sociological perspectives and light on prescriptive advice—perfect if you need a snappy comeback for the "When I was your age, I made my own way" rant you get after asking for a familial loan. Cite structural inequalities and policy failures along with the loss of upward mobility in the "American dream," and no one has to know you're knee deep in credit card bills because of the fancy gym membership you pay for but don't actually use. There are stacks of books on personal finance. Here's our crib sheet.*

- *Gener@tion Debt* by Carmen Wong Ulrich. Title similar to that of Kamenetz's book but with very different advice. The takeaway:

  - The sassy attitude and on-point tips actually make reading about finances kind of fun.
  - Every chapter contains weblinks at the end so you'll have tons of resources at your fingertips.

- *Get a Financial Life: Personal Finance in Your Twenties and Thirties* by Beth Kobliner. The takeaway:

  - It covers the gamut: from how to budget and get out of credit card debt all the way to retirement planning.

---

*You can discreetly tuck these into most purses. (Definitely a good thing in case you happen to lock eyes with a handsome stranger on the subway and don't want him to see you toting some hefty tome with the word "Dummy" or "Idiot" in the title.)

- For the skimmer in all of us, Kobliner considerately ends each chapter with a "financial cramming" page of the most important points.

Find an expert

If you have complicated finances or just like to get a professional opinion, meet with a financial planner and get yourself a game plan. A planner will help you allocate your money in the right places so that you won't be crossing your fingers that Social Security will survive. Being old and alone is one thing; being old, alone, and still in a 600-square-foot walk-up is another, especially because you can do something about the latter. One caveat: Financial planners usually have something to sell you, particularly if they don't charge for their services. If they're associated with one company, for example, they'll be hawking products as part of your plan, even if those products may not be the best for you. When it comes to finding a reputable person, always go to trusted friends and family for recommendations rather than playing eeny-meeny-miney-mo with the Yellow Pages. Expect to spend a couple hundred dollars for a consultation.

Staying liquid

Most financial advisers will tell you that it doesn't make a whole lot of sense to start a savings account while you are carrying debt,* but we suggest having some liquid cash in the event of

---

*If you are up to your ears in credit card debt (and you know who you are), listen to the advisers and put every spare cent into paying down those balances.

179

an unexpected expense, such as needing a new transmission, being in between roommates, or getting canned. By directing a small portion of each paycheck into a savings account, you'll end up with a little fund for emergencies. This money will never hit your checking account, so you won't miss it. Nothing feels as good as paying with cash, and you'll save yourself a ton of interest by not resorting to your cards.

Smart savings accounts
- ✓ Look for no monthly fees, no minimum balance, and the chance to score some interest.
- ✓ Sign up for direct deposit, and you should avoid monthly service charges.

One bank we really like: ING. The no-minimum, no-monthly-fee orange savings accounts have one of the highest interest rates in the country. But the real beauty is that having an account with this Internet-based bank means you won't have an ATM card to tempt you. If you need to access your moolah, you transfer it into your linked checking account, which often takes two to three days. That might be just the lag time you need to realize that a new dress is not quite the emergency you originally thought it was.

2. The '49er, AKA the Gold Digger

Screw saving, I plan on marrying rich

"Marry for money the first time and love the second." Our friend Amber's mom regularly dispenses this sage bit of wisdom. Dads aren't much different. Brenda's father likes to point out, "It's just as easy to fall in love with a rich man as it is a poor man." Talk about eyes on the prize! Marrying for money is so *Dynasty*. Before you count on your Carrington dreams, think about this:

Eight reasons why gold digging is not a smart career choice

1. Most men who marry a trophy either demand a prenup or are wily enough to hide most of their assets, so don't bank on getting half, even if you have his baby.

2. At some point in your life you are going to realize that you sold yourself to the highest bidder—not so good for the self-esteem when you wasted some good years on someone who didn't make you happy.

3. All of the yoga classes, massages, and jewels in the world are no match for a man who will rub Vicks VapoRub on your chest when you are congested.

4. You are hurting all of us smart, independent women and affirming the stereotype of the woman who sees nothing but dollar signs.

5. Not to be too harsh, but if you are trading love for money, well, it sort of sounds like you are taking material goods for sex. Enough said.

6. Guys are onto you. Thank the laddie magazines like *Maxim* for divulging your "secret" way of sussing out whether he's loaded. Natalie, twenty-six, thought her method of asking guys what kind of cars they drive (Nissan Sentra—no! BMW—yes!) and what their favorite vacation spots were (Maldives—yes! Fort Lauderdale—no!) within moments

of meeting them was "subtle." Would you be surprised to learn she's still single?

7. If you're getting money, what do you think he's getting? Probably not a soul mate. If you are happy being a trophy bride, beware the next tournament. Once you get a little older and the sheen wears off, you may be put out to pasture.

8. Money can vanish. Stock markets crash. Companies go under. You know this. If the well runs dry, what are you going to do with some guy till death (or divorce court) do you part whom you don't even like very much?

3. The I'm-Just-Working-Until-I-Get-Married Girl

We're raised to think that we are not complete unless we are married with families of our own, which is very contradictory to what we've been taught about our careers: that we can be anything we want and don't need anyone else to support us. We go to college, get a degree, and bust our asses to move ahead in our career, but there is a tiny part of us that thinks working may not be forever if we're lucky enough to exercise our opt-out option: get married, have kids, and go on leave (or quit for good). Men, on the other hand, are told from the get-go that they'll be dragging their bones to the office every day until retirement, or until a biotech miracle gives them a uterus.

I have a dream . . .
Angela, twenty-six, told us she wants nothing more than to be "the Starbucks Mom," the woman who has a kid but also a full-time nanny. So while the nanny is with the kid, SB Mom can go

to the same Starbucks every morning to catch up with all of her fellow SB-Mom friends, where one can presume they chat in an increasingly caffeinated fashion about just how tough it is to be a stay-at-home mom. In this fantasy, she's also toned from Pilates and home in time to make a lovely meal for her perfect husband and child.

When work sucks—say, your boss threw you under the bus during a meeting or you have been told that thanks to a client request you can kiss your weekend plans good-bye—the idea of staying home and worrying only about your family starts to look appealing. That's because we've left out the part about the cleaning, errands, poopy diapers, and laundry, not to mention the lack of co-workers, adult conversation, and working with a team of like-minded people.

Still think that you are going to get married, quit your job, and live a life of leisure? Think again. In 2002, only 7 percent of all U.S. households consisted of married couples with children in which only the husband worked. Dual-income families with children made up more than twice as many households.[3]

If you know what the Sunday-night blues are or you have a fantasy stay-at-home life, take a look at your career. When people ask what you do, do you answer with "I am an advertising exec" or would you be more likely to say "I work in advertising"? Ask some friends this question. If you are the type to answer, "I am a _____," chances are you are happy with your career choice. How do you identify yourself?

Is your career a pit stop on your road to wedded bliss? Did you choose it based on the number of eligible men you might meet there? Are you working at a job that is beneath you because you don't want to be too successful and intimidating? In

Listen Up, Ladies!

Have an escape route. *Patty, thirty-three, has a sepa-rate savings account that she elegantly calls her "F.U. money." After ten years of being underpaid, overworked, and underappreciated, Patty put her F.U. money to use, quit her soul-sucking job, and started her own business.*

a December 14, 2004, piece in *The New York Times* entitled "Glass Ceiling at Altar as Well as Boardroom," John Schwartz wrote, "Men would rather marry their secretaries than their bosses, and evolution may be to blame." Are you down with this? If yes, read on, because you are . . .

4. The Stop-Here-Add-Spouse Girl

In the board game Life there is a mandatory stop just after you graduate from college. The space says, "Stop Here. Add Spouse." Too many of us are still in a financial holding pattern in our twenties and early thirties, waiting for a ring before we pull the fiscal part of our lives together. In our survey, 60 per-cent of women said that they have either put off or would not consider buying a home until they were married. If you've been saving and living like a real adult, why not get out of your rental and put a stake in the ground? Signing your name to that much debt is daunting, but the tax benefits will probably make it more than worth your while. Many of us hold back on purchasing because the process itself is intimidating. Two steps to get you started:

- **Ask around.** Talk to other homeowners and get a referral to an agent or broker.

- **Read up.** One book we have found to be particularly helpful is *The Single Woman's Guide to Real Estate* by Donna Raskin and Susan Hawthorne. Their book goes step-by-step through the buying process, including whether or not to buy at all, in an empowering but not annoying "chick book" kind of way.

You may not be the first to get hitched, but you may be the first to build equity.

Stop here. Add spouse? Not for Meaghan

Meaghan moved home after college because, as she puts it, "I wasn't about to blow money on rent in the city." She contributed a hefty part of her paycheck to an IRA and a savings account and after two years had saved $20,000. Not bad considering that she was earning a magazine editor's salary, not an investment banker's. Because Meaghan is a savvy sister, she knew that as a first-time home buyer she could use the money in her IRA to help with a down payment without incurring any penalties. She admits that this was before the crazy housing boom of the early 2000s, but still, it's more doable than you may think. So with her $20K she had a down payment on a small apartment—beyond the five boroughs. "Sure, it was a compromise—I had to commute to the city—but it had a little yard, and it was mine. The thing that was so funny was that I was dating a guy at the time—we had been together for two years—and we broke up the day I closed. (Good thing, since his brother-in-law was my attorney and had waived all the closing fees!)" Going from living with Mom and Pops and having her laundry done for her to having to pay a mortgage caused Meaghan to go through a period of "Holy shit, I'm really on my own. Buying a place just forces you to grow up. I had to keep a job to make sure I could pay my mortgage—now I had something to lose."

Meaghan sold that place a few years ago and is now in a bigger, better apartment closer to the city. Buying that little place when she was young got her into the game and gave her a "she really has her stuff together" vibe. She says, "Some guys I've dated assume that my parents must have bought it for me and that makes me so pissed. I've never taken a handout from anyone. I'm no trust-funder. I saved the money I was earning and

Believe It or Knot

In the last decade, single women in the United States have been outbuying men when it comes to homes. Twenty-one percent of single women purchased a place in 2005, compared to only 9 percent of single men.[4]

didn't buy stupid things. I just have this real need to be self-sufficient. I know that whatever happens—I could have kids, someone could leave me—I'll always have this asset to fall back on."

If you think owning a home makes you intimidating to men, consider your hand officially slapped. Please do not buy into the idea that men would prefer to marry their secretaries (thank you very much, Mr. Schwartz). If you are reading this book, you are not the kind of girl who is going to want to be with a man who can't handle your successful self. You worked way too hard to get where you are.

If he is not confident enough to handle your financial success, do you really think he's enough of a man to be a good husband or father? An insecure man is a dangerous thing. Can someone this insecure handle your male friendships? How about your next promotion? The man worth your time is going to love that you are shrewd enough to be a home owner, and if he doesn't, you should toss him. Seriously, how exhausting would it be to play the ditzy wifey who bakes a mean pie but can't balance her checkbook?

5. I Am Woman, Hear Me Roar

Are you sick of hearing that women put their life on hold waiting for a ring? Don't be shy about your financial acumen. If you have a home, max out your 401(k), and are moving up in your chosen career, you have an obligation to show your credit-challenged friends the error of their ways. You know that it's annoying to hear them bitch about their debt as they order their daily tall decaf soy lattes. Tell them what they're doing wrong. Help a sister out.

HOW FINANCIALLY FIT ARE YOU?

Now you know that getting hitched because you want to quit your job (or just get rid of your twelve-year-old Hyundai) is a recipe for disaster. Getting into that 5-series on your own will feel much better anyway. Do you know the ABCs of finances? We're no econ majors, but one can learn a lot from the school of bounced checks and high interest rates. Take this quiz and find out what your financial fitness score is.

1. **Question:** If you buy a pair of shoes for $200 with a credit card that charges 20 percent interest and you pay only the minimum due each month ($5), how long will it take to pay off those shoes and how much would you end up paying?
   Answer: It will take you five years and five months to pay off that charge. You will have paid $122 in interest, making the actual cost of those shoes $322. Thank you to CNN Money for helping us out with that one![5]

2. **Question:** If Joan starts to contribute to her 401(k) at twenty-six at a rate of 3 percent and Vivian waits until she is thirty but contributes 6 percent, who will have more money in ten years?

   Answer: Who cares? The point is that you should start putting money away *today.* Not next week, next month, or when you turn thirty. If your employer offers matching funds and you are not taking advantage of that, you are turning down free cash. The money is taken out of your paycheck before tax, and we promise that you won't miss it. As you get raises, increase the percentage you contribute. You can use this money to buy a home without being penalized, and you will be amazed at how quickly it accumulates.

3. **Question:** What impacts your credit score most: falling behind on payments, maxing out your credit cards, or having multiple lines of credit open even if you owe only a little bit on each of them?

   Answer: All three are bad and will ding your credit score, causing potential lenders either to refuse your request or to offer you a loan, but with a sky-high interest rate. The best thing to do? Keep your balance far from your limit. Just because you can charge a new car on your Visa doesn't mean you should. Close down any lines of credit you don't need.

KEEPING YOUR CREDIT IN CHECK

- Enroll in autopay so you have one less thing to think about. If you prefer to make the payments yourself and you know that a payment is going to be a couple of days late, call your creditor and let them know the situation and when they can expect a check.

- Potential lenders look to see how strapped you are by seeing how close you are to your credit limit. If your limit is $20K and you are up to $18K, you look like someone who is in over her head.

- Lenders also look at how much trouble you can get yourself into. You may not carry a lot of debt, but if you have five credit cards open, each with a limit of a couple of thousand dollars, your profile says you have the potential to get into serious debt quickly.

4. **Question:** How much do all of your bills add up to each month? (Quick—no grabbing for statements.)

   Answer: Don't know? Figure it out. We aren't saying that you have to have a crazy tight budget and know exactly how much money you should be spending on, say, food each week (though if you do, kudos to you), but you should have a ballpark estimate of what's coming in and going out. Knowing your regular expenses will clue you in to your discretionary income without sweating whether or not the gas company is going to shut it off for real this month.

5. **Question:** How much does your bank charge you for a bounced check?

  Answer: This is a trick question! You should have no reason to know the answer to this question. Why? Because (a) you always know how much is going in versus coming out so you don't bounce checks! and (b) you're enrolled in an overdraft protection program through your bank. Paying $35 because you overdrew your account by $10 is a heartbreak. Really, it is.

6. **Question:** According to the powers that be, what percentage of your gross income should your monthly rent check be?

  Answer: Your rent should be no more than one third of your gross pay (before taxes are taken out).

7. **Question:** You realize you aren't going to be able to pay off your credit card this month for the first time in a long time, when your best friend calls you and invites you to Rome, where she will be apartment-sitting for a month. All you need to pay for is the airfare. Should you go?

  Answer: Whip out the plastic and buy a ticket (coach, of course). Check out the last-minute fares and online specials, take a week off work, and go! Getting further into debt is not great, but when are you going to get the opportunity to live in Rome for free again? Try to save where you can, though. Make meals at home. Buy food for picnics. Live like a local, skip the touristy restaurants, and limit your souvenir buying, so that you don't end up paying off those Sistine Chapel snow globes for the next two years.

There is such a thing as good debt. Education can be good debt, except if you're practicing massage with your master's and Ph.D. degrees. Travel is often good debt. By travel we don't mean a weekend in Cancún. When a once-in-a-lifetime opportunity comes up, jump on it! But if you're going to Rome only to sightsee at Prada, Gucci, and D&G, skip it. That's not the enriching travel experience we're talking about.

8. **Question:** Fill in the blank, when April 15 rolls around, I feel _____.

   Answer: Hopefully, the word you thought of wasn't a synonym for "worried." Some people like to have as little taken from their check as possible, i.e., "I would rather invest my money than give it to Uncle Sam until tax time." That's fine if you are a hard-core investor. We say it's better to have as much withheld as possible each pay period. That way when tax time comes around you are guaranteed a nice little nest egg for your IRA (or to pay off credit card bills), rather than the "Yikes, where am I going to come up with $2,000 to pay the federal government?" moment.

9. **Question:** When it comes to clothing, there are some items you can buy cheaply and nobody will be able to tell, and others where you have to go with quality. What is the one area in which you aren't fooling anyone with your H&M picks?

   Answer: Shoes and handbags: expensive, classic accessories (or funky shoes and purses) can make an outfit. Although if you're really low on funds, today's purse knockoffs are pretty damn good and can save you a mint in the long run. A cheap shoe is not only easy to spot but tends to be less comfortable in the long run. Luxury brands usually cost more because they were made by skilled leather workers in Italy, not poor children in Asia. Check out the clearance racks at department stores for deals on good-quality shoes or splurge on one pair of killer heels that'll go with almost everything.

10. **Question:** What percentage interest is your savings account earning?

Answer: Another trick question! If you read this and thought, "What savings account?" tsk, tsk. You can set up a savings account to automatically draw as little as $20 from each paycheck. It may not seem like much, but having around $500 per year in a savings account is better than a kick in the head. And you won't notice the $20 because you will never have had it in the first place.

11. **Question:** What is the fastest growing nonviolent crime?

Answer: Identity theft. An amendment to the Fair Credit Reporting Act requires each of the nationwide consumer reporting companies—Equifax, Experian, and Trans-Union—to provide you with a free copy of your credit report, at your request, once every twelve months. Go to www.annualcreditreport.com to get yours. Many other websites claim to offer "free credit reports," "free credit scores," or "free credit monitoring." But be careful. These sites are not part of the official annual free credit report program and often charge monthly fees.

12. **Question:** What is the highest APR that you are currently paying?

   Answer: If you read this and thought, "I have no idea," chances are it's high. Assuming that your credit is in good shape, you shouldn't be paying an APR much over 9.9 percent. Give your credit card company a call and request a lower rate. And try to get a fixed rate, not a variable one, since a 7.9 percent introductory rate could go up to prime interest rate plus 12 percent within the year. Call other card companies if you are unable to negotiate a lower rate, or search online for a card with a lower rate and transfer your balance (however, beware of hidden transfer fees). Sometimes just threatening to transfer a balance will get your current company to suddenly "find" a lower rate for you.

13. **Question:** What is your salary negotiation style?

   Answer: If your style goes beyond "How much are you offering me? Okay, I'll take it!," bravo. It's an unfortunate truth that women shortchange themselves all the time because we're socialized that being assertive in negotiating is unfeminine and "pushy." We care a little too much about interpersonal relationships at work and forget that at the end of the day, we're still line items in our boss's budget.

   Here are the best negotiation tactics:

   1. Do your homework. Know what you're worth. The most powerful moment is when you are accepting a new job

offer. Translate your experiences (and contributions during review time) into something you'll see on your pay stubs.

2. Don't get personal. *Do not* ever ask for more money because of personal needs.

3. Don't take the job-well-done praise and a jovial relationship with your boss as a substitute for a fair increase.

4. Don't take no for an answer. You don't have to be agro and demand more cash or you walk. Approach it as a "Gee, can't we put our heads together and come up with something more suitable to my experience?" Schedule a check-back-in-three-months review, or ask for in-kind extras (more vacation days, company cell phone, flextime) if your boss won't budge on the bottom line.

5. Learn to use silence. Don't cave in when the other person gets quiet after you've presented your case. He or she is expecting you to feel uncomfortable and agree to anything to end the discomfort. Your silence is a classy way of showing that you disagree.

6. Never feel pressured to take what's offered in the moment. Say you appreciate it and that you'll think about it.

If you either got a couple of these wrong or skipped the quiz altogether because you know that you are a financial fiasco, pull your head out of the sand and get yourself together. You know the feeling that comes after you *really* clean your apartment? That's how it feels when you have your finances in order: a place for everything and everything in its place. When you know where you stand and have a plan for the future, it's easier

Being sure-footed financially means that buying gifts for three B2Bs in one summer won't send you into an overdraft free fall. The Bridal Wave years are chock full of anxiety inducers beyond your control (hello, Grandma Innya Bizness). Your checkbook balance is not one of them. You have the power.

to decide what to buy and what not to buy, and sometimes that means yes, you can spend a couple of C-notes on a timeless sweater without the postpurchase guilt.

You know the drill by now; just to be sure that we guilt you into following our advice, please place your right hand on that handbag you just had to have (and are *still* paying off), and repeat the following:

I promise to take responsibility for my financial future. I understand that even though sorting through my finances and creating a budget is not superfun, it is something that I will stop putting off for some day in the future. I under-

stand that waiting for a rich relative to die and leave me an inheritance does not count as a financial plan. When I don't find exactly what I am shopping for, I will not buy myself a pity gift of perfume or a random makeup item. I will know the APR of each credit card in my possession, and I will use the cards only in the case of a true emergency. I understand that needing a bikini wax is not an emergency, neither is a manicure or a 50 percent off sale. I will discuss finances with friends and ask them for referrals or tips, but I will then research those tips myself and not blindly follow a friend's financial advice, especially if the word "pyramid" is mentioned. I will become an avid reader of my city's free weekly paper in search of free/cheap weekend activities (don't knock the Tofu Festival till you've tried it). I will stop playing into the tired stereotype that women can't manage their money. I will forge ahead with my life and not wait for marriage to achieve any goal that I may have. I will get myself in order so that when I do meet someone I will have something to offer other than an encyclopedic knowledge of restaurants where dinner for two costs half my monthly rent.

CHAPTER 9

Wake Up and Smell the Bouquet

> You've got a great guy and you're on the track to
> Wedding-ville: how to tell if your relationship
> is ready for the trip

Considering that 88 percent of Americans marry at least once in their lifetime,[1] it's safe to say that if you want to get married, you probably will. Maybe not to the guy you're dating now and maybe not according to when it was "supposed to happen," but someday, and hopefully for the rest of your life. But before you begin your very own Ring Watch, take the time to be sure that your relationship is as ready as you are. You'll save yourself a heap of heartbreak down the road.

Don't Be in the Dark in the City of Light

Kate was on vacation in Paris with her live-in boyfriend of four years, Paul. Paris, the city of light, the setting of countless romance novels, a place where even people who don't like each other very much could fall in love. Before leaving, Kate told her friends she was sure she would return with a ring. She packed as if she were decorating a set. She had the perfect backdrop and the perfect wardrobe. She was going to have a great story to tell: "There I was, gazing out at the Seine, with Notre Dame in the distance, watching the sun begin to set, when Paul got down on one knee and asked me if I would be his wife." At every romantic landmark, she prepared herself for Paul to pop the question, playing the scene in her head. They went to the Luxembourg Gardens, the Louvre, the Champs-Élysées, the Pont-Neuf, but no dice. Toward the end of their stay, just as Kate was about to give up hope, they went to the Eiffel Tower. As they were taking in the views, Paul turned to Kate, and nervously cleared his throat. Kate almost blurted out "Yes!" before he said a word. She held her breath, waiting to hear those four words: "Will you marry me?" Instead what she heard was "I can't do this anymore." There on the observation deck, surrounded by kissing tourists, he dumped her. Turns out, he just didn't see their relationship moving forward. But it wasn't her, it was him. As if that would make her feel better. He just wasn't ready for this kind of commitment. Nice, buddy.

Now, we agree that Paul should have been tossed off the tower for his timing and tact, but at least he was honest in the end. The most disturbing part of Kate's scenario is not the fact that she is now abnormally distressed by the sight of berets and can't order a crepe without feeling overly emotional, but that the two of them had no idea where the other's head was. How could they be in such different stages of the same relationship? The answer is easy: *lack of communication*. Kate just assumed that Paul wanted what she wanted, and Paul was too scared to let Kate know that he had been having serious doubts. When it comes to maintaining a healthy relationship, communication is a must.

You may finish each other's sentences, you may be able to read his mood by the lines on his forehead, but you still need to "check in" every now and then to make sure that you are both on the same page of your relationship. No, not an every-day, anxious "Are we happy?" harping, but a once-in-a-while "Are we both feeling the same way about our relationship?" check-in. Think of it like getting your car's oil changed. Sometimes it's a pain to do, and hey, everything's been running just fine, but if you wait too long, when something does go wrong, it may be too far gone to fix.

How Checking In Saved Seema from Heartache

Seema was laid off from her job and found herself having to reevaluate her five-month-old relationship. The only thing keeping her in Nashville was Joel, and Seema didn't want to be "that girl"—the one who stayed somewhere just for a guy she hoped might someday be as serious about her as she was about him, *if* she stuck it out for long enough. So Seema took the direct approach and flat-out asked Joel if he saw a future together. When he said he did, she set about her Nashville job hunt in earnest. The good news was that she was offered her dream job. The bad news? It was in North Carolina. "When I got the job, I bawled my eyes out because I didn't know what to do. We sat down, and he assured me that we would be able to get through it—it would be a temporary thing, and it was important for me to keep moving forward in my career. It was hard to leave because I was so happy with my life. Before I made my final decision, I asked him more specifically if he saw us getting married and he said, 'Yes.' Now we're in a committed long-distance relationship, and while I don't know when he'll propose, at least I know I'm not completely wasting my time."

Way to go, Seema! She and Joel were able to have difficult conversations and make decisions as a team, based on what made sense for both of their careers and personal growth. Even though she is wondering *when* he will propose, she is not waiting around wondering *if* the thought's ever crossed his mind.

The Danger of Assumptions: Learn from Sara and Mark

Sara and Mark had dated off and on throughout college and in the years following. After a brief split they got back together just after Sara had made up her mind to move to Chicago, a place she had always wanted to live. Mark was not as excited about the cross-country move but didn't want to break up, so he packed his things and headed east. Since they were both new to the city and broke, they ended up moving in together to save money (*never* a good idea, by the way). For Sara, moving in together was a precursor to an engagement: "I figured that if we lived together for a year, we would get engaged and then married. I mean, we had been together for seven years, so what else was there?" Sara had set a timeline that she never discussed with Mark, and in her eyes everything was going according to plan. Since neither of them ever talked about their relationship, she had no reason to think otherwise. After a year of living together, Sara began to talk about rings. Their engagement was less than romantic: Mark never exactly "asked," but he did cough up the dough to buy the ring that Sara designed for herself on adiamondisforever.com. They got married after a lackluster, yearlong engagement. But they never made it to their first wedding anniversary. Mark had his own meltdown and realized he had never really wanted to get engaged or married. He was just going along with things because it seemed like the easiest thing to do. Chalk up two more to the starter-marriage stats.

If you are in a long-term relationship you think might be headed for the altar, *do not:*

- **Move in together to save money or for some other "practical" reason.** Mark and Sara's decision to move in together was purely a rational one. Sure, you spend nearly every night at his place and your heart breaks with every rent check you write, but that isn't a reason to cohabitate. Moving in together is serious business. Just like getting married too early, moving in may break a relationship that wasn't really at the right stage. If you are looking to save some dough, get a roommate or move to a smaller, less expensive place.

- **Take the path of least resistance.** Mark was going along for a ride that he had never wanted to take. He loved Sara and didn't want to upset her or end their relationship, but he definitely wasn't ready to hop on the betrothed bandwagon. In fact, his desire to avoid conflict turned into a train wreck. It's easy to coast along in a relationship when someone else is making all the decisions, but only you live your life and at some point your true feelings are going to come out. Better to let the truth flow before the guests have arrived at your wedding. The sooner you are honest about your feelings, the less mess you will have to clean up.

- **Assume that living together means you'll get married.** Sara thought that when Mark decided to move cross-country for her and sign a lease with her, it was a sign that he saw their future together the way she did. Little did she know that all he saw was one less fight and cheaper rent. In our experience, women almost always assume that sharing house keys means that marriage is soon to follow as long as they pass some unspoken compatibility test, while many guys think that living together is just living together.

- **Live in your own bubble.** Sara was blindsided by Mark's realization, clueless as to how he had been feeling. All this heartache could conceivably been avoided with one "Are you happy? Am I happy?" check-in.

- **Mistake the length of a relationship for its viability.** Longer doesn't always mean better. So you have been with a guy for ten years and he asks you to marry him. Your answer might not be a given. There is a difference between ten years and the rest of your life. While not the preferred response, you can ask for some time to think about your answer after a proposal. He took his time to come to his decision and got to pick his moment to pop the question; why should you have to answer on the spot? (Oh, and if it happens on a JumboTron, say "yes" to avoid public humiliation and then, as you kiss him in front of tens of thousands of people, whisper in his ear, "Let's talk after the game.")

Before you find yourself selecting a china pattern or deciding between tulips and lilies for your reception, every couple needs to sit down and cover the basics. To be truly marriage-minded, you and your man need to discuss family, finances, faith, children, where you'll live, and, yes, sex. If you can't broach these topics with him, you've got no business traipsing into Tiffany's with him to try on rings.

In the Bedroom

Talking about sex (in a non-phone-sex way) is not sexy. It is, however, a necessary conversation to have before you get hitched. When Jenny moved in with Todd, she had no idea that he was such an avid reader—of porn! "He was always weird about his closet. I thought that he was just very organized, but one day when I was looking for a box of books that I hadn't seen since the move, I looked in his closet and found an enormous stack of *Penthouse* magazines." Jenny was freaked out. She'd had no idea that Todd was into porn. She told him what she had found and that she was not cool with it. "I told him that it made me feel like I'm not enough for him." He explained to her that the collection had been his late father's, and that while he never looked at the magazines, he also couldn't bring himself to throw them out. We're not sure we buy that, but the point is: in order to deal with your feelings, you need to know the whole story. Good for Jenny for telling Todd about her discovery. If she hadn't said anything, it would have gnawed at her. "Every time I went out with friends, I would have wondered if he was at home surrounded by his stash."

Nobody wants to ask a question that they don't want to know the answer to, like "Am I satisfying you sexually?" But it's better to find out about his penchant for handcuffs now than on the night of your honeymoon. And don't forget to look out for number one, *you*. Are you getting what you need in the bedroom? Are you hoping that once you're married he will be more, uh, generous in the sack?

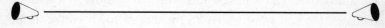

Among the many things that getting married won't accomplish is transforming a so-so sack mate into a stud.

All this stuff might sound like common sense, but it's amazing how many couples don't have conversations about the most basic aspects of embarking on a life together. Whether they are afraid of bringing up a potential deal breaker or simply worried about ruining an otherwise perfect evening, couples often avoid discussions that could prevent them from becoming a starter-marriage statistic. Don't even think about taking the plunge until you've run through the following checklist.

Do

✓ **Get married for the right reasons.**

Do both of you believe in marriage? Do you both want to get married? To each other? Is one of you more ready than the other? We are not advocating talking things over to death, but you both have to be ready to take the leap at the same time. Getting married is not going to make everything better. It will only illuminate existing problems.

Don't

✗ **Get engaged or married because it's what comes next.**

Just because you live together or have been together for a certain amount of time doesn't mean that your relationship is marriageworthy.

Do

✓ **Have an honest conversation about what you want for your future.**

Do you know that you do not want children? Or do you imagine a brood of ten? Will you raise them according to a specific religion? Do you want to live in the city or town you're in for the rest of your life, or does he think that marriage means moving to the suburbs, your idea of hell on earth? Will you be expected to go to both parents' holiday celebrations? Sure, these questions aren't exactly sexy or romantic, but if you and your man haven't discussed them, you're setting yourself up for some major drama down the line. Trust us, these questions are actually way more important than "So, do you want a big wedding or a small one?"

Don't

✗ Lie to him or to yourself.

If he tells you he doesn't want kids, he means he doesn't want kids. Don't think that he will change his mind after a few years or after he sees how great you are with kids or how great your sister's kids are. If he's told you that he plans on his mother moving in with the two of you once you buy a place, don't tell yourself that once you have a "Mrs." in front of your name, he's going to ditch Ma because you tell him to. Likewise, if you have a burning desire to leave your job to follow your true love, say, motocross racing, you should mention that before you walk down the aisle.

Do

✓ Get ready to compromise.

He takes an annual weeklong golf trip with his brothers. You don't think it's fair that he uses his precious little vacation time on a getaway with his brothers when you are neither invited nor interested in going even if you were. Learning the art of compromise to find a solution that can work for the both of you is key to keeping a partnership on an even keel. Maybe the annual golf trip will become an every-other-year thing. Maybe next year the trip will be in a place you have always wanted to visit yourself. Maybe the golf week will become a golf weekend.

Don't

✗ Lose your backbone.

Compromise is great, but if after a compromise you feel like the only one who gave something up or you feel angry about the compromise, something is amiss. Giving up your girl's night out because your fiancé hates to be alone is not a compromise. Giving up your male friends because your boyfriend is jealous is not a compromise. Giving up a dysfunctional friendship with a toxic ex who treated you terribly and never paid back all the money he "borrowed" because your boyfriend thinks he's a self-ish bastard is a compromise. A compromise will leave both of you happy: you see *Lord of the Rings* in the theater (again), and he goes shopping with you for your cousin's baby's birthday present. That's what we call a compromise.

Do
✓ **Love each other for your faults.**

Plug your ears because you may not want to hear this cliché for the millionth time, but it bears repeating: *People don't change.* The things your boyfriend does that totally annoy you are not going to stop after you slip the ring on his finger. Trying to change somebody is a waste of time and energy. The tough part is figuring out which faults you can live with, which are too much for you to handle, and what's fixable. Leaving the toilet seat up? Fixable. Leaving you stranded at the airport because he's "too busy" to pick you up? Not. One woman may find her boyfriend's tendency to flirt with other women completely un-acceptable, while another women may find it harmless so long as he is not taking the flirtation to a physical level. Make a list of his faults and separate them by those that you can live with and those that you cannot.* While you're at it, make a list of

---

*When you're finished, destroy this list. Do not just throw it out. Shred it, burn it, or even eat it. Better yet, keep it digital. Don't name the file "eddie's_pros_and _cons_Rev 3," and delete from your hard drive when done.

HINT

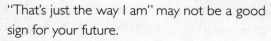

"That's just the way I am" may not be a good sign for your future.

your own faults. You may find that you both have some room to improve.

Don't

✗ **Live with shortcomings that affect your life negatively.** This may also sound obvious, but abuse of any sort, be it physical or emotional, is not all right. If your boyfriend's actions cause you to feel bad about yourself, *dump him*! If he has a problem with drinking or drugs and refuses to get help: *cut and run*! Marriage is a support system, and you should feel safe, cherished, and loved in your relationship. If you have any concerns about your safety or well-being, get help immediately. If he's worth keeping, he'll seek the counseling and treatment he needs.

Do

✓ **Run a credit check.**

Okay, maybe not an *actual* credit check, but what you want to avoid is a surprise $50K worth of debt in your name. Getting married to someone means getting married to his financial past. That's not to say that his being in debt would be a deal breaker, but you should have all of the facts before entering into such a potentially costly union (especially if you live in a no-fault divorce state!). You should know what he earns, what

209

his amount of debt is, and if he has any black marks on his credit history. Applying for a mortgage together is not the best time to find out that your man defaulted on his school loans. And beyond the past, what about his future? Does he have a 401(k)? A savings account? Does he live within a budget? And if he doesn't, is he open to the idea? Do you expect to have a joint checking account, or will you continue to keep some of your earnings separate? Does he have a "my money is my business" attitude? (By the way, this could be a red flag that he doesn't view marriage as a partnership.)

Don't

✗ Base your decision to get married on finances.

Translation: Don't marry for money! Just. Don't. Do. It. Yes, that woman on the street with her LV bag and Manolo Blahniks is stylin'—but does she really look happy? At the end of the day you need a man who will rub your tired feet, not just foot the bill. The last word on marrying for dough: Don't take his word for what kind of assets he has. He may be one of those "Surprise! This was all bought on credit, and now we have to abscond to Mexico to avoid the creditors, but hey, won't it be an adventure?" kind of guys.

Do

✓ Review Chapters 1–8

Review the previous chapters in this book and ask yourself if you are heading to the altar due to any of the pressures that we have outlined: Sick of being on the receiving end of the IGBN call? Want a better answer for the next time you're asked, "So when are you two going to tie the knot?" Tired of being called to the dance floor to catch the bouquet? Too scared to eat dinner alone? Think all the problems in your relationship will be solved when you get married? Do you think that a husband will somehow make you more whole as a person?

Don't
   ✗ **Confuse a wedding for a marriage.**

Getting married because your timeline is getting tight, because you want to wear that sample-sale Vera Wang you got "just in case" before it goes out of style, because you are on vacation and it seems like a fun, spontaneous thing to do, or because you think that's what you do after a certain amount of time in a relationship, will leave you with a beautiful wedding album and a not-so-beautiful divorce.

You're Rocking the Rock, but Will You Do the I Do?

You've checked off everything on the list above, and you're sporting a shiny rock on your left hand. It's a shoo-in, right? Maybe not. The number of engagements that never make it to the altar is higher than ever before. Now, that may not be a bad thing. One wedding planner we consulted told us, "Now that the starter-marriage phenomenon is so well known, couples are terrified of becoming a statistic. Also, because so many people in their twenties and thirties grew up with divorced parents, they don't want to make the same mistakes as their moms and dads, so they're more likely to call an engagement off before the invites are in the mail."

211

In Kayleen Schaefer's *Details* article "The Epidemic of Broken Engagements," she wonders if getting engaged is the new going steady. The idea got us thinking: Is giving someone an engagement ring a way of taking her off the market, a branding that says, "She's taken"? If so, why haven't women come up with their own way of letting everyone know that their guy is spoken for? Say, a "Back off, he's mine" band. De Beers, are you listening?

So You're Engaged; Is That Any Reason to Get Married?

It's never too late to put the brakes on an engagement. Just because your guy has popped the question doesn't necessarily mean that you should get married, even if you said, "Yes"! Here are the top ten signs that your engagement will not (or should not) make it to the church on time.

1. **You got engaged after dating for less than three months.** Except in rare instances, there is no way you can know somebody well enough to make such a big commitment. What's the rush? If you know it's right at three months, it should still be right in six months or a year.

2. **The engagement came after an ultimatum.** Nobody wants to get engaged under duress.

3. **"How am I going to get out of this one?" was the first thought that popped into your head right after you said "Yes."** Everyone looks at her fiancé at some point and wonders, "Am I making the right decision?" but that

feeling goes away. If yours doesn't, it could be your gut telling you that you're about to make a big mistake.

4. **He asked you in public, and what else could you do?** We aren't sure why guys think that putting you on the spot in front of everyone you know is a good idea. It is one of life's great mysteries.

5. **One of you or both of you has no interest in the planning of the wedding.** Our wedding planner extraordinaire told us that one sure sign that something is awry in a relationship is when the couples don't move the planning forward.

6. **You cannot imagine a life with him.** If your picture of the future doesn't include him or has him relegated to the periphery of your life, he may not be the right one for you. Or maybe you just aren't that into marriage.

7. **You keep postponing the date.** The length of engagements has increased over the years, in part so people can plan ever more lavish nuptials and engagements that are really "going steady" statements. If you keep pushing the date of your wedding back, it may be a sign that you are not ready to get hitched.

8. **You are way too excited about getting married "on time."** If you are more into the idea of making your timeline than marrying your boyfriend, chances are you're getting married for the wrong reasons. Do not pass "Go." Pay Chapter 4, "The Timeline," another visit, please.

9. **All of your friends and family think it's a bad idea.** Anyone can grin and say through clenched teeth, "As long as he makes her happy." If your loved ones can't muster up these seven words, something is wrong.

10. **He doesn't let you be you.** If you have to tiptoe around your guy or hide any part of your true personality, you are not ready to get married to him. Sure, you can be who he wants you to be for a certain amount of time, but a lifetime? That's no fun at all.

Till death do you part is a long, long time. Hopefully, when you head down the aisle, your head will be on straight.

Repeat After Us

I promise to check in with my partner every now and then, just to make sure that our relationship is working for both of us and that we are both moving toward the same goals. I promise to do this in a mature and not reactive or insecure, worrywart kind of way. Before accepting an engagement ring I will know whether or not my man has been audited by the IRS, hates children, plans on quitting his job after we get married to focus on his "art," or is on the FBI's Most Wanted List. I will not try to change him beyond his unfortunate tendency to wear front-pleat slacks. I will not ban sports from our weekends or certain friends from his life. I promise to work on compromise and loving him even for his most annoying attributes, like his habit of leaving wet towels on the bed. I will listen to my gut instincts, and if that means breaking off the engagement days before the wedding, I will do that and I will be proud of myself for doing so as long as it doesn't make the front page of a newspaper à la the Runaway Bride.

We've Come a Long Way, Baby

Like any natural disaster, the element of surprise is part of what makes the Bridal Wave so hard to deal with: a perfectly lovely Thanksgiving can, with one "Maybe you're just being too picky" comment, turn into a Bridal Wave Danger Zone. But the biggest surprise is how forcefully the Bridal Wave hits when you get to a certain age, no matter what else is going on in your life.

You can't predict exactly when the Bridal Wave will crash into your life, but you can be prepared for when it does. By now you should have all of the tools you need to get you through these years without being knocked down and thrown face-first into the sand. You may even be ready to lend a hand to other potential Bridal Wave victims.

Every woman's In Case of Emergency (ICE) kit should contain these five items:

- 1 honesty scale
- 1 pair lobridemy blinders
- 1 self-reliance stun gun
- 1 friendship safety net
- 1 bitch-tinguisher

Wage your battles with the honesty scale. A very important skill we hope you've honed is knowing when to lie (a *white* lie, of course!) and when to be honest. A little fibbing may be necessary when it comes to receiving someone else's good news or when your real feelings will cause you to be a scene stealer in the worst way. Honesty is the best policy when in a one-on-one situation with a pressure source like a family member, a rude interloper, a good friend, or a boyfriend. Be honest when you want to make a difference or change someone's mind. Ask yourself: Will being honest affect the way this person interacts with me or other women? If the answer is a resounding *no,* play nice and roll your eyes when they've left your line of sight. Then commiserate and share your true feelings with a fellow BW survivor and move on.

Put on the lobridemy blinders. Yes, your friend is a boring B2B, stuck in a wedlock headlock, totally obsessed with herself and her impending nuptials. Yes, you would rather pluck your arm hair than play another bridal shower game, but you love your friend, and (surprise!) this isn't about you. It's about her. You wouldn't be invited if she didn't count you as a friend. Your presence was requested because someone wants you to share in her happiness (or, in the case of a Frenemy, rub her happiness in your face). Use our tips for saving cash and your sanity at these affairs, pal around with someone to make it less painful, and choose to have fun (or else fake it really, really well).

Zap yourself with your self-reliance stun gun. The Bridal Wave strikes right when you are supposed to be getting your own stuff together, and too many women go off course on the great manhunt on account of all the marriage pressure.

Don't wait around for Mr. Right when you could be getting together a down payment for your own place because your well-deserved promotion has finally put you in the majors. You're never going to get your young, single self back again, so why not make the most of it? This is *your* time to experiment and learn what would make you a happier person. Once you start refocusing your efforts on you, instead of why you're alone, why he isn't proposing, or why everyone you know has already beat you to the bridal shop, you'll be on your way. And the truth is, the more you focus on the things you can control, the less the other stuff is going to affect you.

Never forget your friendship safety net. At some point, you may fall off the Bridal Wave high wire perched precariously over the Crazy Pit, so you are going to want a safety net: your friends. Lean on them during these years. Clueing people in to how you feel is the only way you'll gain their support. Your friends aren't mind readers and may not even say the right thing when you're in the thick of it, but real emotional camaraderie doesn't always have to be expressed through words. Know who you can count on and who you can't.

Use your bitch-tinguisher. As much as we talk about the women in your life that you count on like family during your single years, we still have to acknowledge the less-talked-about aspect of female friendships: competition and the way it can pit us against one another. It's time to call a truce and use the I STOLE YOUR BOYFRIEND T-shirt as a dust rag. Let's stop keeping other women down and start supporting one another.

Changing Tides

Ah, to be a modern woman. Isn't it just fantastic? We'll go to speed dating, silent dating, blind dating—we'll have a one-night stand and promise to call *really* soon or give him a fake number—we'll pay our own way and open our own doors—but there is one area that hasn't changed that much: the marriage gambit. One minute we're pulling all-nighters to get ahead at work (and using $65 concealer to hide the fact), the next minute we're held captive in a country club, sitting around sighing over someone's stemware as if it's the culmination of everything a chick could ever want. Whether we're asked to submit to the voluntary subservience of bridesmaidom or we're waiting for our guy to get to The Question already, the Bridal Wave years are probably the first time we've been confronted with such overt throwbacks to "feminine" passivity. No wonder it makes us nuts!

When we're smack in the middle of Bridal Wavus Overwhelmus, we have a lot of trouble seeing the Big Picture through all the Big Days. Take a look at these stats about the state of the modern woman. They might surprise you.

"Aren't there more weddings than ever?"

Reality check: The number of weddings each year is decreasing.

- Between 1960 and 2004, the number of unmarried couples in America increased more than 1,200 percent.

- In 1960, there were ninety married couples for every co-habiting couple. By the year 2010, if the present trend continues, there will be seven married couples for every cohabiting couple.

The fact that all statistics point to the decline of traditional life paths has caused the Wedding Industrial Complex to effectively stage an all-out wedding propaganda blitz (as if you hadn't noticed). This $100 billion industry will continue to thrive only if it can sell us on the idea that first comes love, then comes the big rock, followed by the engagement party, the shower, the bachelorette, and finally The Most Important Day of Your Life (oh, don't forget the postwedding brunch). Don't be a sucker. Marriage is more than a marketing concept.

"Having a baby-by-bank is sooo depressing!"

Reality check: Forty percent of women in their twenties would consider having a baby on their own if they reached their mid-thirties and had not found the right man to marry,[1] and 54 percent of female high school seniors say they believe that having a child outside of marriage is a worthwhile lifestyle, up from 33 percent in 1980.[2]

Based on these numbers, going to the sperm bank will no longer be considered another walk of shame or a last resort because you couldn't find a man. As Jennifer Egan's *New York Times Magazine* article "A Few Good Sperm" points out, some women feel that choosing to be a single mom can actually alleviate a lot of the pressure to marry the first person who comes along with enough testosterone to father a child.

"If I'm too successful, I'll never find a man!"

Reality check: Give the dudes some credit. In 2003, 30 percent of working wives earned more than their husbands. And looking at recent trends in higher education, it's safe to say that the antiquated mode of thinking that men would prefer to marry their secretaries will be on life support soon. After all, by 2009, demographers predict, women will earn 58 percent of all baccalaureate degrees awarded in the United States.[3] Not only have we come a long way, baby, but we're also leaving the boys in the dust.[4] Check out these numbers:

Degree	1971 (% of Women Earning)	2001 (% of Women Earning)
Medical	9%	43%
MBA	4%	41%
Law	7%	47%

At this rate, guys are going to start marrying us for *their* financial security (or applying to be our secretaries)! Of the 187 participants in *Fortune's* Most Powerful Women in Business Summit in 2001, *30% had househusbands*. And of the 50 women on the 2002 list, more than one third have a husband at home either full- or part-time.[5] We don't know about you, but most of the men in our lives would jump at the chance to quit the nine-to-five slog for a while. Maybe marriage in the twenty-first century can finally be about finding the yang to your yin—a person who complements your needs and goals.

As women populate higher positions in the workforce, we are poised to have greater and greater influence in our culture, everything from the way in which we are marketed to, all the way to workplace child care options.* The key is not "being one of the guys" but remembering that we are women. Let's use our power to effect change to make the workplace better suited to *our* needs.

"Everyone I know is coupled up but me!"

Reality check: In 2010, 30 percent of homes will be inhabited by people who live alone.[6] Put another way, that's almost one in three people.

Not only are you not alone, but along with your fellow singletons, you make up an incredible political force. In fact, in 2008, unmarried women will make up the largest single demographic group.[7] First things first: read the papers and have a stake in the world by voting. Secondly, if you really don't know *anyone* else who isn't matched up like cake toppers bound for Noah's Ark, you need to meet some new people. Seriously.

A fat lot of good all this may do you now, but these shifting paradigms could have a major impact in coming years on our ideas about marriage—and, we can only hope, on the insane pressure society places on women.

---

*Hello, family values! Why isn't child care a mandatory benefit like health insurance?

Good News and Bad News

The good news is that there is an end in sight. One day the invitations will stop trickling in, and your life will stop revolving around marriage-everything. The bad news is that this is not the last challenging time period you will face. Just when you think it's safe to go back in the water, the next wave will strike: the Baby Wave! If you think a lobridemized friend droning on is a drag, get ready for the baby voice: You are so cute, yes you are, yes you are. Who's mommy's wittle man? Did you make a poopy? Trust us, you'll be longing for the day your friend asked your opinion about tea length versus full length!

Crazy Is Normal. We're All Crazy. So We're All Normal

You *should* feel certifiable now—this is a crazy time in your life, everything is up in the air. Someday, when your life is more settled, you will actually miss the days of nuttiness, uncertainty, and possibilities. Stop thinking "Everybody I know is . . . , so what the heck is wrong with me?" The answer is simple: *nothing!* So keep your head up and roll with the crazies—just don't marry them!

All right, we couldn't let you go without making some final sanity-saving vows. It's a long list, but you still have to say it out loud (unless you're on a bus or something, because then you'll just look weird).

Repeat After Us

I, _____, take myself as I am. I understand that I cannot control how other people behave, but I can control how I react to their rudeness. I cannot control the fact that my boyfriend is a loser, but I can recognize it and move on. I understand that the only real "wasted time" is time when I am unhappy and not doing anything to change that. I will not deem a relationship a failure because it doesn't end with a trip to the altar, because life is about the journey and not the destination. I promise to live every aspect of my life to the fullest, because life is too short to settle for anything less than that. Settling today will only lead to a dreary existence, because I will always wonder "What if?" I understand that the cliché that you need to love yourself before you can love someone else is true, and though I can look in the mirror and find a million things I would like to change, I will also try to find what I would never trade for any amount of money. I understand that everyone has issues with themselves and comparing myself to someone else is a waste of time. And for all I know, that perfect couple I see every morning walking their dog really hate each other. He could be cheating on her and she could be thinking "I made a huge mistake." I will trust my gut when it come to major decisions in my life because my gut reaction tends to reflect my true feelings better than my mind because my gut cannot rationalize. So I take myself for better and for worse, from this day forward.

ACKNOWLEDGMENTS

There are so many people without whom this book would literally not exist. First, to each and every one of the 450+ women who took our online survey and shared their stories with us, we thank you. Our fantastic editor Julia Cheiffetz, who believed in this book from Day 1. We also wish to acknowledge the sleep deprivation she suffered in service to our manuscript and hope she heads somewhere tropical and completely unwired very soon. We owe so much to Christine Earle at ICM, for immediately understanding this project and working tirelessly to make it see the light of day; the amazing Donna Brodie and The Writer's Room NYC; JoAnn Schilb for her expertise on so many levels; Megan O'Toole for her Web savvy; Cheri Messerli for her fantastic illustrations; and the supercool Rebecca Thienes. Everyone at Random House, especially Lisa Barnes, Lynn Buckley, Diana Franco, Laura Goldin, and Beth Pearson. For their early words of support and advice, we are indebted to John Searles, Celeste Perron, and Andrea Lavinthal, as well as to our readers Jessica O'Toole, Jacque Lynn Schiller, and Sabena Budke, for making the book better and more true. We also want to thank our friends and colleagues: Mary Buckley, Liz Brixius, Brian Brooks, Jodi Coppernoll, Tracey Creech, Tom Donovan, Susan Glatzer and Tad Greenough, Robin Holland, Jonathan Hum, Raymond Hwang, Jodi Kanger, Anthony Kaufman, Kathleen Kindle, Vivian Ko, Suzanne Kisbye, Noah and Susannah Laracy, Karen Leavitt, Jennifer Leung, Andrea Meyer, Lily Oei, Patrick O'Neal, Geraldine Patawaran, Carla Parks, Devin Snell, Courtney Tolman, Matt Torneo, Dave Weaver, Jeannie Uyanik, Cathy Yacoub, Farley Zeigler, and all the women at TBWA\Chiat\Day as well as some former and current *Cosmo* girls: Jane Katz, Meaghan Buchan, Brooke Le Poer Trench, Amy Grippo, and of course, Kate White.

From Val:

Thanks to my sister and best friend, Dr. Catherine Cabrera, for making sure that my maiden name made it onto the cover. My dad, who, by putting the pressure on Tommy, took some of the pressure off me. My mom, whose love of bad jokes and punning made me who I am today for better or worse. My parents as a couple, who have provided me an example of a healthy, loving relationship for over thirty-one years. Tommy, whose understanding, encouragement, and selflessness continually blow me away. And I'd like to thank Erin. We've been through a lot, and I could not ask for a better partner in crime.

From Erin:

Thanks to my Golden Girls Emily Peluso and Cheryl Richard. My parents, for providing so much fodder over the years in a house full of chaos and laughter. My mom, who stopped with the marriage talk as soon as she realized she was going to be all over the book, and my dad, who kept going, undeterred. My brothers, Joe, Mike, and Patrick, who taught me how to throw down long before I knew about makeup, and my new sisters, Gabriela and Lisa (one benefit to the bros' tying-the-knot thing), Aunt Carol and all the Torneos; Aunt Gail and all the Cassarinos; Nicole Conlon, for my earliest example of pursuing something you love. Joe, Barbara, Louie, Bela, Abby, and most especially Sascha, for everything and for always. To Val, I'd like to say I couldn't have done this without you, and why would I have wanted to?

NOTES

CHAPTER 1: "I'VE GOT BIG NEWS!"

1. "The Wedding Planner: History of Wedding Traditions," KOKO Oklahoma City 5, www.channeloklahoma.com/wedding/2399764/detail.html (accessed May 30, 2006).

CHAPTER 2: LOBRIDEMIZED!

1. Shane McMurray, "Wedding Market Overview," The Wedding Report, www.theweddingreport.com/us.html#about (accessed May 30, 2006).

2. Shane McMurray, "2006 U.S. Basic Wedding Cost," The Wedding Report, www.theweddingreport.com/us.html#about (accessed May 30, 2006).

3. Fairchild Bridal Group, "The American Wedding," Sell the Bride, www.sellthebride.com/documents/americanweddingsurvey.pdf (11) (accessed May 30, 2006).

CHAPTER 3: NAVIGATING WEDDING SEASON

1. U.S. Census Bureau, 2002, as cited in Radio Advertising Bureau, "Instant Background Report for Bridal Market" (2005).

2. Marg Duncombe, "Words and Phrases," Backroads Touring Company, www.backroadstouring.co.uk/phraseorigins.htm (accessed November 10, 2005).

3. "Bridal Couple Showers," Bridal Showers, www.prescottweddings.com/archivejik.html (accessed November 10, 2005).

4. "The Knot and Kohl's Unwrap the Ultimate Rules on Wedding Gifts," Kohl's Corporation, www.kohlscorporation.com/2005PressReleases/News0520Release.htm (accessed May 30, 2006).

CHAPTER 5: THE LEAGUE OF CONCERNED CITIZENS

1. Sara Williams, "Mistletoe," About.com, http://landscaping.about.com/gi/
dynamic/offsite.htm?zi=1/XJ&sdn=landscaping&zu=http%3A%2F%2
Fgardenline.usask.ca%2Fmisc%2Fmistleto.html (accessed February 1, 2006).

CHAPTER 6: REALITY CHECK

1. John Maltby, Liza Day, Lynn E. McCutcheon, Raphael Gillett, James
Houran, and Diane D. Ashe, "Personality and Coping: A Context for Exam-
ining Celebrity Worship and Mental Health," *British Journal of Psychology* 95,
no. 4 (2004): 411.

2. Associated Press, "Tori Spelling Reportedly Ending Marriage," MSNBC,
http://msnbc.msn.com/id/9398955/ (accessed May 30, 2006).

3. Approximate cost based on details of the wedding given in Gina Serpe,
"A 'One Tree' Wedding," E! Online, www.eonline.com/News/Items/
0,1,16359,00.html (accessed May 30, 2006).

CHAPTER 7: SPINSTER CITY

1. Stephanie Armour, "U.S. Workers Feel Burn of Long Hours, Less Leisure,"
USA Today, http://usatoday.com/money/workplace/2003-12-16-hours-cover
_x.htm (accessed February 1, 2006).

2. Carl T. Hall, "Study Speeds Up Biological Clocks. Fertility Rates Dip After
Women Hit 27," *San Francisco Chronicle*, www.sfgate.com/cgi-bin/article
.cgi?file=/chronicle/archive/2002/04/30/MN182697.DTL (accessed
January 30, 2006).

3. National Vital Statistics System, "Indicator 12: Life Expectancy," Life
Expectancy Tables, www.efmoody.com/estate/lifeexpectancy.html (accessed
March 19, 2006).

CHAPTER 8: A SHOULDER TO LEAN ON, NOT A BANK ACCOUNT TO SPONGE OFF

1. "Surviving Divorce: How to Protect Yourself Financially," NYSSCPA
.org, www.nysscpa.org/sound_advice/money_1.06.03.htm (accessed
May 30, 2006).

2. "Poverty Rate Rises, Household Income Declines, Census Bureau Reports," *United States Department of Commerce News*, September 24, 2002,
www.census.gov/Press-Release/www/2002/cb02-124.html (accessed
May 30, 2006).

3. "Traditional Families Account for Only 7 Percent of U.S. Households," Population Reference Bureau, March 2003, www.prb.org/Template.cfm ?Section=PRB&template=/ContentManagement/ContentDisplay.cfm& ContentID=8288 (accessed May 30, 2006).

4. Stephanie Rosenblum, "For Men, a Fear of Commitment," *The New York Times,* www.nytimes.com/2006/02/12/realestate/12cov.html?ex =1297400400&en=2b4cf673b97e06dd&ei=5088&partner=rssnyt& emc=rss (accessed May 30, 2006).

5. "When Will You Be Debt Free?" CNN Money.com, http://cgi.money .cnn.com/tools/debtplanner/debtplanner.jsp (accessed May 30, 2006).

CHAPTER 9: WAKE UP AND SMELL THE BOUQUET

1. Susan Breslow Sardone, "Wedding & Honeymoon Statistics," About.com, http://honeymoons.about.com/cs/eurogen1/a/weddingstats.htm (accessed December 21, 2005).

CONCLUSION: WE'VE COME A LONG WAY, BABY

1. Michelle Conlin, "Unmarried America," *Business Week,* October 23, 2003, p. 106.

2. Ibid.

3. Jennifer Delahunty Britz, "To All the Girls I've Rejected," *The New York Times,* www.nytimes.com/2006/03/23/opinion/23britz.html?incamp =article_popular_4 (accessed May 30, 2006).

4. Peg Tyre and Daniel McGinn, "She Works, He Doesn't," *Newsweek,* May 12, 2003, p. 44.

5. Betsy Morris, "The New Trophy Husband," *Fortune,* October 14, 200' p. 78.

6. Michelle Conlin, "Unmarried America," *Business Week,* October 2? p. 106.

7. Ruy Teixeira, "Unmarried America: Demographics and Attitudes, Women's Voices, Women's Votes, www.wvwv.org/mediaroom/vier .cfm?id=71 (accessed May 30, 2006).

PHOTO: © JO ANN SCHILB

ABOUT THE AUTHORS

ERIN TORNEO (above, right) is a writer based in New York. A former editor at *Cosmopolitan,* she has written for *Lucky, Variety, The Independent, The Kyoto Journal, SEED,* and *indieWIRE.* Although she lives with her boyfriend, she still checks the "single" box every time she fills out a form, because there's no "in-a-committed-relationship-and-just-fine-with-things-the-way-they-are-but-I-probably-wouldn't-say-no-if-he-asked" option.

VALERIE CABRERA KRAUSE (above, left) is a writer and pop culture junkie living in Los Angeles. Previously, she was an account planner for the advertising firm TBWA\Chiat\Day. Although she didn't have a date to her prom, Val lucked out in love and married the first guy she dated for longer than two months.

How They Know Each Other

Erin and Valerie met as college freshman and endured ing bouts of singledom together. After sharing an apartment meant for one person, they backpacked through Sout While they never lived together again and in fact mov site coasts, Val and Erin remain good friends. Erin wedding.

3. "Traditional Families Account for Only 7 Percent of U.S. Households," Population Reference Bureau, March 2003, www.prb.org/Template.cfm ?Section=PRB&template=/ContentManagement/ContentDisplay.cfm& ContentID=8288 (accessed May 30, 2006).

4. Stephanie Rosenblum, "For Men, a Fear of Commitment," *The New York Times,* www.nytimes.com/2006/02/12/realestate/12cov.html?ex =1297400400&en=2b4cf673b97e06dd&ei=5088&partner=rssnyt& emc=rss (accessed May 30, 2006).

5. "When Will You Be Debt Free?" CNN Money.com, http://cgi.money .cnn.com/tools/debtplanner/debtplanner.jsp (accessed May 30, 2006).

CHAPTER 9: WAKE UP AND SMELL THE BOUQUET

1. Susan Breslow Sardone, "Wedding & Honeymoon Statistics," About.com, http://honeymoons.about.com/cs/eurogen1/a/weddingstats.htm (accessed December 21, 2005).

CONCLUSION: WE'VE COME A LONG WAY, BABY

1. Michelle Conlin, "Unmarried America," *Business Week,* October 23, 2003, p. 106.

2. Ibid.

3. Jennifer Delahunty Britz, "To All the Girls I've Rejected," *The New York Times,* www.nytimes.com/2006/03/23/opinion/23britz.html?incamp =article_popular_4 (accessed May 30, 2006).

4. Peg Tyre and Daniel McGinn, "She Works, He Doesn't," *Newsweek,* May 12, 2003, p. 44.

5. Betsy Morris, "The New Trophy Husband," *Fortune,* October 14, 2002, p. 78.

6. Michelle Conlin, "Unmarried America," *Business Week,* October 23, 2003, p. 106.

7. Ruy Teixeira, "Unmarried America: Demographics and Attitudes," Women's Voices, Women's Votes, www.wvwv.org/mediaroom/view_news .cfm?id=71 (accessed May 30, 2006).

PHOTO: © JO ANN SCHILB

ABOUT THE AUTHORS

ERIN TORNEO (above, right) is a writer based in New York. A former editor at *Cosmopolitan,* she has written for *Lucky, Variety, The Independent, The Kyoto Journal, SEED,* and *indieWIRE.* Although she lives with her boyfriend, she still checks the "single" box every time she fills out a form, because there's no "in-a-committed-relationship-and-just-fine-with-things-the-way-they-are-but-I-probably-wouldn't-say-no-if-he-asked" option.

VALERIE CABRERA KRAUSE (above, left) is a writer and pop culture junkie living in Los Angeles. Previously, she was an account planner for the advertising firm TBWA\Chiat\Day. Although she didn't have a date to her prom, Val lucked out in love and married the first guy she dated for longer than two months.

How They Know Each Other

Erin and Valerie met as college freshman and endured varying bouts of singledom together. After sharing an apartment in Japan meant for one person, they backpacked through Southeast Asia. While they never lived together again and in fact moved to opposite coasts, Val and Erin remain good friends. Erin cried at Val's wedding.